Teachers
Mentoring
Teachers

Teachers
Mentoring
Teachers

A
PRACTICAL
APPROACH
to Helping New
and Experienced
Staff

John C. Daresh

CORWIN PRESS, INC.
A Sage Publications Company
Thousand Oaks, California

For information:

Corwin Press, Inc.
A Sage Publications Company
2455 Teller Road
Thousand Oaks, California 91320
www.corwinpress.com

Sage Publications Ltd.
6 Bonhill Street
London EC2A 4PU
United Kingdom

Sage Publications India Pvt. Ltd.
B-42 Panchsheel Enclave
Post Box 4109
New Delhi 110 017 India

Printed in the United States of America

Library of Congress Cataloging-in-Publication Data

Daresh, John C.
Teachers mentoring teachers: A practical approach to helping
new and experienced staff / John C. Daresh.
    p. cm.
Includes bibliographical references and index.
ISBN 0-7619-4575-X (C)—ISBN 0-7619-4576-8 (P)
1. Mentoring in education. I. Title.
LB1731.4 .D375 2003
371.102—dc21

                                    2002010112

This book is printed on acid-free paper.

02 03 04 05 06 10 9 8 7 6 5 4 3 2 1

Acquisitions Editor:	Robert D. Clouse
Editorial Assistant:	Erin Clow
Associate Editor:	Kylee Liegl
Production Editor:	Diane S. Foster
Copy Editor:	Kris Bergstad
Typesetter:	C&M Digitals (P) Ltd.
Proofreader:	Scott Oney
Cover Designer:	Tracy E. Miller
Production Artist:	Janet Foulger

Contents

Acknowledgments   vii

Dedication   ix

About the Author   xi

1. **Mentoring: A Welcome Teaching Assistant**   1
    Why Start a Mentoring Program?   1
    Benefits to Mentors   3
    Benefits to Protégés   4
    Benefits to Districts   5
    Potential Problems With Mentoring   5
    Summarizing the Chapter   7

2. **Initial Program Development**   8
    Planning a Program: A Typical Case   8
    Mentoring Planning Team: Setting the Stage   9
    Implementation: Putting It All Together   10
    Appraisal: How Did It Work?   11
    Summarizing the Chapter   12

3. **What Is Our Purpose?**   13
    Decide the Target Groups   13
    Two Cases   14
    Identifying a Purpose   15
    Checking Your Plan   17
    Summarizing the Chapter   18

4. **Who Is a Mentor?**   20
    Characteristics of Mentors: One Case   20
    Characteristics of Mentors: A Second Case   22
    Are Good Teachers Always Good Mentors?   23
    What Are Some Characteristics of Effective Mentors?   24
    Danger Signals   25
    Responsibilities of Mentors   26
    Checking Your Plan   27
    Summarizing the Chapter   27

5. **Preparing People to Serve as Mentors**   28
    Domain 1: Orientation to Mentoring   28
    Domain 2: Effective Planning and Managing of Instruction   29

Domain 3: Human Relations Skills   31
Domain 4: Mentor Process Skills   33
Domain 5: Local Implementation Issues   35
Checking Your Plan   36
Summarizing the Chapter   37

6. **Matching Mentors and Protégés**   38
A Case of a Bad Match   38
Mentor Matching: Some Myths   39
So What Should You Use?   40
Some Additional Thoughts   41
Checking Your Plan   42
Summarizing the Chapter   43

7. **What Do Mentors Do?**   44
A Case in Point   44
Additional Responsibilities of Mentors   48
Developing an Action Plan   50
Checking Your Plan   50
Summarizing the Chapter   52

8. **Mentoring for Beginning Teachers**   53
Beginning Teachers' Needs   55
A Case Study   56
How Could Mentoring Help?   57
Summarizing the Chapter   62
References   62

9. **Mentoring for Veterans**   63
Mentoring for Veterans: Two Cases   63
Mentoring for Experienced Transfers   66
Mentoring for Veterans Within a System   66
Checking Your Plan   67
Summarizing the Chapter   67

10. **Did the Mentoring Program Work?**   69
Evaluation Questions   69
Checking Your Plan   73
Summarizing the Chapter   74

11. **Moving Beyond Starting Your Mentoring Program**   75
How Does Professional Development Fit?   76
Reviewing Local Priorities   76
What Happens After Mentoring?   77
Checking Your Plan   77
Summarizing the Chapter   78

Appendix A: Answers to the Mentoring
    Background Quiz in Chapter 1   79

Appendix B: Mentor-Protégé Action Planning Form   81

Suggested Readings   83

Index   85

ACKNOWLEDGMENTS

The last few years have witnessed a steady decline in one of the most precious resources that any nation can possess. Fewer and fewer people want to take a walk down the road that leads them to a life in the classroom. And among the things that we must have in this nation are strong schools. Strong schools, in turn, depend upon a steady infusion of committed teachers ready to take on the challenges of working with students.

Social analysts have a number of theories to explain the reduction of apparent interest in teaching. For example, a strong economy in the past few years may be making some professional roles more financially appealing than service in a school. As this book is being completed, that vigorous economic scene has diminished, but the need for new teachers seems to continue. Others might claim that people are shying away from teaching because the pressures and stress associated with the job are no longer acceptable to most people. Kids are too disinterested in schooling; parents are more demanding . . . the list includes endless examples of frustrations familiar to educators. Regardless of the possible explanations for the waning interest in teaching as a profession, however, the facts are clear. Teachers have never been rich, and teachers have always faced challenging students, parents, communities, and other similar obstacles. But potential teachers have been "in the wings" ready to step in to take up the responsibilities of educating America's youth.

So why the change now? Perhaps one of the reasons serves as the underlying rationale for this book. Despite the stress of teaching, there may be some ways in which the educational community can begin to build a kind of support infrastructure that will make it more likely that people see the teaching profession as a place where success is truly possible. A big part of that infrastructure is related to the need for more effective and focused approaches to professional development for teachers. No longer can we simply say that each year teachers are given three or four "staff development days" to acquire new skills or get rid of bad habits. Professional development must be conceived of as a continuing process that presents new and veteran teachers with insights into how to make their lives in classrooms more productive and less stressful. Developing and maintaining mentor programs for teachers may be such a strategy to ensure ongoing opportunities for professional and personal growth and increased satisfaction. There may, in fact, be ways to make teaching an appealing profession if we work at solutions rather than only identifying problems.

Thanks go out to many for serving as inspirations and for assistance in the preparation of this work. First, I thank the hundreds of excellent classroom teachers who have been my colleagues throughout the past thirty-plus years as an educator. I have been honored to meet some of the most caring and thoughtful educators in the world as I have worked in Ohio, Colorado, Illinois, and now Texas. One thing that I have learned in my travels is that dedication to the needs of children is an international phenomenon, and I have been able to witness so much kindness and concern over the years. There are a lot of great mentors out there!

I was prompted to write this book by a pair of current colleagues who read some of my other work on mentoring for school principals and decided that I might be able to share a few thoughts as they relate to teachers. Specifically, I note my good friend and colleague at the University of Texas at El Paso, Sandra Hurley, now serving in the Dean's Office, but always a classroom teacher at heart. The other person who "bugged" me is Micaela Varela, a student in our graduate courses and an excellent teacher in the El Paso Independent School District. Her interest in finding ways to help her coworkers in "the trenches" made me believe that a book like this would be important.

I thank my colleagues in the College of Education at the University of Texas at El Paso, notably Robin Hughes, Susan Rippberger, and Rudy Rincones, who have all encouraged me and been patient with the idiosyncrasies associated with colleagues writing a book. Josie Tinajero, our dean, has also been most helpful, as have the leadership team of the University. Thanks to all!

Finally, I express my thanks to Robb Clouse and Kylee Liegl at Corwin Press. These two, as well as so many others in Thousand Oaks, have become not only great professional associates over the past few years, but good friends.

To
Bridget and Stephanie

ABOUT THE AUTHOR

 **John C. Daresh** is Professor of Educational Leadership and the Director of the Principal Preparation Program at the University of Texas at El Paso. He has worked in faculty and administrative positions in higher education for more than twenty years at the University of Cincinnati, The Ohio State University, the University of Northern Colorado, and now in Texas. Daresh has served as a consultant for school districts, universities, and state departments of education across the United States, Europe, Africa, and Asia. Over the years, he has authored more than 100 articles, books, book chapters, and papers dealing with professional development for educators. He began his career by working in private and public schools in Dubuque, Iowa, and Chicago. He received his doctorate from the University of Wisconsin at Madison.

Mentoring 1

A Welcome Teaching Assistant

This chapter describes what mentoring is and what it can do for your school system and for the people who teach in your classrooms.

Mentoring is an ongoing process in which individuals in an organization provide support and guidance to others who can become effective contributors to the goals of the organization. Unlike some conventional views of mentoring, the stance I take in this book is that a mentor does not necessarily have to be an older person who is ready and willing to *pass down* wisdom and *provide all of the answers* to those who are newcomers. Usually, mentors have a lot of experience and craft knowledge to share with others. But the notion that good mentoring consists of a sage who directs the works of the less experienced to the point that assurances are made that no one will make any mistakes is not reasonable. Being a mentor implies the responsibility of not only sharing, but also of listening and learning. If your school or district adopts a mentoring program, the program must have the potential of helping those who are mentored (or *protégés*, a word that will be used throughout this book), those who serve as mentors, and also the school system that chooses to start the mentoring program.

Before reading the remainder of this chapter, you should complete the Mentoring Background Quiz. This quiz is designed to help you in assessing your understanding of this topic. (Answers to the Quiz may be found in Appendix A).

The remaining chapters of the book will (a) help you gain a more complete view of what mentoring is, (b) explore some of the major issues associated with planning, implementing, and evaluating a mentoring program in your district, and (c) provide you with practical advice that is meant to make your program an important part of the professional development program for teachers in your school system.

WHY START A MENTORING PROGRAM?

If your district chooses to adopt a teacher mentoring program, a strong commitment will be needed to support this effort. This effort does not

MENTORING BACKGROUND QUIZ: TRUE OR FALSE?

_____ 1. Mentor-protégé relationships are always more beneficial for the protégé than for the mentor.

_____ 2. Individuals with more years of experience in a certain job make better mentors than individuals with fewer years of experience.

_____ 3. Participating in mentoring relationships contributes equally to career advancement and professional development.

_____ 4. Women tend to value mentor-protégé relationships more than men do.

_____ 5. Participating in a mentoring relationship motivates both parties involved to participate in future mentoring relationships.

_____ 6. For a mentoring relationship to work, both the mentor and the protégé should believe that the relationship is a very close one.

_____ 7. Having only one mentor is the best form of support for a protégé.

_____ 8. A healthy mentoring relationship should not experience any problems or difficulties.

_____ 9. Matching mentors and protégés should be based only on the fact that both individuals have the same position.

_____10. Mentoring relationships are vehicles for job enrichment and professional development.

_____11. Reading books, participating in institutes, and attending conferences can be a part of effective mentoring.

_____12. Mentoring relationships are separate and distinct from other types of supportive relationships that might be found in organizations.

_____13. Individuals who are perceived as being good at their jobs will always be perceived as good mentors.

_____14. At times, both the mentor and the protégé may expect too much from the mentoring relationship.

_____15. Mentors are people who should always be able to provide the "right" answers.

(Answers to these questions are provided in Appendix A)

necessarily imply the need for a lot of money, however. In fact, over time, a district with a mentoring program for teachers can actually save money by retaining newer teachers (and avoiding the need to keep recruiting to fill the same positions over and over) and, in some cases, identifying teachers with difficulties at a point before drastic measures must be taken for nonrenewals. On the other hand, time must be devoted to mentor training, development, and opportunities in order for mentoring to take place. Initiating a program also means that a district accepts the fact that investing in the development and professional growth of teachers is worthwhile.

If mentoring implies changing attitudes and improving skills, time, commitment, and some financial support, why should you even consider this type of program? After all, most people recognize that change in education is often extremely difficult to achieve, that time is the least available resource for educators, and that few districts have a lot of extra cash lying about. Despite these obstacles, however, quality school systems promote mentoring programs because of the many benefits for teachers, and those benefits are likely to be realized by mentors, protégés, and school districts.

BENEFITS TO MENTORS

At some point in your life, you have probably experienced an informal process in your relationship with someone, and that process might be described as mentoring. Your mentor might have been a favorite teacher in school, an athletic coach, an employer, or any other person who might have made a difference in your personal or professional life. And you have probably had a similar impact on the life of another person. You may have also served as a mentor.

Before you read about the common benefits to those who serve as mentors, take a moment to reflect on some of the values you have personally derived from serving as a mentor to others.

_____

_____

_____

_____

_____

_____

_____

Now, compare your list with some of the benefits presented in the literature on this topic:

1. After serving as mentors, people report greater overall satisfaction with their jobs as teachers. (Like any good teacher, a mentor learns as much, if not more, as those who are mentored.)

2. Mentors get increased recognition from their peers. (People who get a reputation of being effective organizational helpers usually achieve a higher status in the system.)

3. Mentoring gives people opportunities for personal career advancement.

4. Mentors often gain a renewed enthusiasm for the profession. (Mentors often find that the things they frequently take for granted become behaviors that are highly valued by others.)

In short, people who have served in a mentoring capacity to teacher colleagues report that they have gained much in this type of relationship. Perhaps the best way to summarize this feeling is to say that despite the amount of time involved in maintaining effective mentoring relationships, mentors express a desire to serve in this capacity again in the future.

BENEFITS TO PROTÉGÉS

You have likely been at the receiving end of a mentoring relationship at some point in your life as well. What are some of the benefits that you have enjoyed as a result of someone serving as your mentor?

_____

_____

_____

_____

_____

_____

Individuals who have been protégés in formal mentoring programs for teachers have identified the following benefits:

1. Protégés feel more confident about their professional competence. (They find that others respect their work.)

2. Protégés see theory translated into practice. (They learn that it is possible for good ideas to be transformed into effective actions on the job.)

3. Communication skills are enhanced. (Mentoring relationships lead to the creation of a climate of collegial support across the whole district.)

4. Mentoring is a way to learn the "tricks of the trade."

5. Mentoring makes people feel as if they belong. (It makes people feel as if others care about their personal and professional well-being.)

In general, mentoring relationships—whether they evolve naturally through informal contact with someone (such as mentoring from a favorite teacher) or develop through a structured and formal program (such as mentoring for the beginning teachers in a school district)—are powerful learning opportunities. Protégés learn more about their professional lives and gain more insight into their personal needs, visions, and values than through any other kind of learning experience.

BENEFITS TO DISTRICTS

School systems also gain from the implementation of mentoring programs for classroom teachers.

What are some of the benefits that you see as possible for school districts that adopt mentoring for teachers?

_____

_____

_____

_____

_____

_____

_____

School districts across the United States have explored mentoring schemes for teachers and have identified the following benefits:

1. They have more capable staff. (Teachers in school systems that have mentoring programs tend to be energized by this practice.)

2. An attitude of lifelong learning is created among all teachers.

3. Higher motivation levels and job satisfaction are found in the staff. (More effective and enthusiastic professional performance results when people understand that the system demonstrates that employees are worthy by establishing a mentoring program.)

4. Teachers demonstrate an improved sense of self-esteem.

5. Greater productivity results. (All of these other benefits are realized, people do their jobs better, and the organization is more productive.)

POTENTIAL PROBLEMS WITH MENTORING

Despite the great number of benefits that are likely to be achieved by mentors, protégés, and school districts, potential problems also need to be understood. Some of these problems are listed below. There are also some ways in which the problems might be minimized. These problems are listed to make you aware of them, not to discourage you from implementing a mentoring program for your teachers.

Potential Problem 1: Relationships that are too protective and controlling might be formed.
- *Possible Solution:* At the outset, both the mentor and the protégé need to specify the precise level of support that is needed during the term of the mentoring relationship.

Potential Problem 2: Mentors who become advocates for their protégés might begin to ignore real limitations.
- *Possible Solution:* Mentors must constantly keep in mind that they are to support and help people in a realistic way—not create perfect, heroic images of their protégés.

Potential Problem 3: Mentors might become too demanding of the individuals with whom they work.
- *Possible Solution:* A learning contract or other form of written agreement can be prepared at the outset of the mentoring relationship as a way to encourage the specification of expectations on the part of the mentor and protégés.

Potential Problem 4: Good teachers do not always make good mentors.
- *Possible Solution:* School districts that establish mentoring programs must be careful to avoid the tendency to promote mentoring as a form of recognition or reward for teachers. Mentoring is hard work and implies a commitment to a special approach to teaching that goes beyond simply reacting to others' questions.

Potential Problem 5: Protégés might develop a limited perspective on problem solving by relying too much on a single mentor.
- *Possible Solution:* Protégés should be encouraged to find and work with multiple mentors.

Potential Problem 6: Protégés might develop too great a reliance on particular mentors.
- *Possible Solution:* Districts can establish teams of mentors and encourage protégés to select different individuals for different skills that are found in the total team.

Potential Problem 7: Expectations that are established for mentoring relationships might be unrealistically high.
- *Possible Solution:* Open communication at the outset between mentors and protégés, along with the development of a formal guide or contract to guide the relationship, is essential.

Potential Problem 8: Mentors and protégés often form very close relationships that eventually will end. Both parties are likely to feel a great sense of loss and pain.

- *Possible Solution:* Mentors and protégés need to talk to one another openly about the formation of long-term friendships that grow from the mentor-protégé relationship. Mentors and protégés quickly become equals, and with that development, partnerships that are based on parity might last for entire careers.

SUMMARIZING THE CHAPTER

This opening chapter provided a brief overview and orientation to the concept of mentoring as it can be used in your school system to support teachers. Mentoring has the following characteristics:

- Mentoring is a powerful device that may help teachers develop new insights into the profession. This is true whether talking about experienced or new teachers.
- Mentoring may reduce isolation and can build a collegial network among professional colleagues.
- Mentoring helps move the novice teacher from a level of mere survival to initial success when used with beginning teachers. When applied to experienced teachers, mentoring can be a way for professionals to develop a sense of renewed enthusiasm for their jobs and for enhanced commitment to the profession of education.

2 Initial Program Development

Once you have decided to start a mentoring program in your school district, you need to address a number of key issues. Whenever any new program (such as a mentoring program for classroom teachers) is to be incorporated into a school system, certain preliminary activities must take place in order for the program to be accepted by school personnel—thus increasing the likelihood of being successful. This chapter includes information that you can use as you begin to plan a mentoring program. In addition, it presents an outline to assist you and other planners of local mentoring programs for classroom teachers with program design, implementation, and evaluation efforts.

PLANNING A PROGRAM: A TYPICAL CASE

Grace Chen was given the responsibility to develop a mentoring program for the teachers of the Bridgeport Valley Independent School District. The district had never devoted so much attention to the improvement of staff professional development in the past, so assigning someone to this task was a real change. Michael Daniels, the new district superintendent, had indicated that staff development was to be given high priority. The problem was that, despite the new interest in mentoring, Grace was now faced with carrying out a task for which there was little previous direction. Also, Daniels wanted a plan for the program on his desk as soon as possible.

If you were Grace, what suggestions would you make for dealing with this assigned task?

_____

_____

_____

_____

One of the things that could be done to make the Bridgeport Valley mentoring program into an effective venture would be to realize that Grace cannot do the job all by herself. She might be able to coordinate a program once it is off the ground, but the first thing that should occur is to bring together a planning team to work with Grace on her assigned task. The mentoring planning team might consist of the district personnel director, the district curriculum coordinator or coordinator of staff development, representative teachers who are likely to serve as mentors, and perhaps representatives from the local community. If you were asked to put together a committee in your district to be responsible for planning a mentoring program for teachers, who would you include as members?

_____

_____

_____

_____

_____

_____

_____

The composition of the Mentoring Planning Team must be unique to each school district and should be based on local concerns, priorities, conditions, and realities.

MENTORING PLANNING TEAM: SETTING THE STAGE

Before you set up a mentoring program for the first time in a school district, outline the main components of the plan (its definition, purpose, and goals). Once your district has decided to adopt a mentoring program for your teachers, it needs to develop an implementation plan. Your plan might address the broad categories that are noted in the following overview outline, or it may take on another form that is appropriate for you and your district. Additional information regarding the various points is addressed in subsequent chapters of this book. Always remember, however, that whatever direction you take in planning a mentoring program for the teachers in your district, the most critical issue to consider at the outset is, "Why do we want to develop a mentoring program?"

  I. Definition
      A. Are the terms clearly defined?
      B. Are the terms as defined used consistently throughout the plan?

II. Purpose, rationale, or philosophy
   A. Is there a statement of purpose for the plan?
   B. Is the purpose statement compatible with the following:
      1. The school board's philosophy of education and the mission statement adopted by the district?
      2. The professional development plan for the district?
   C. Are the fundamental reasons for the adoption of a mentoring program stated?
   D. Does the rationale include statements of belief concerning areas that are related to mentoring?
   E. Is the rationale compatible with state or national trends, and the school board's stated philosophy of education?

III. Goals and objectives
   A. Are broad program goals and objectives written?
   B. Are the goals and objectives compatible with
      1. Each other?
      2. The school board's philosophy of education?
      3. The district's mission statement?
      4. The district's plan for professional development?
      5. The purpose and rationale for the mentoring program?
   C. Does the plan include provisions for mentors and all other teachers to set individual objectives?

IMPLEMENTATION: PUTTING IT ALL TOGETHER

After the stage has been set through careful planning, you can begin the implementation process. Some of the major issues that need to be addressed at this point are (a) mentor selection, (b) mentor training, (c) mentor assignment, (d) matching system roles and responsibilities, and (e) target groups. The following outline gives an overview of these issues:

IV. Mentor selection
   A. Are eligibility requirements for becoming a mentor stated?
   B. Are procedures and criteria for nominating and selecting mentors stated?

V. Mentor training
   A. Is orientation planned for the mentors?
   B. Is there a plan to have preliminary training for new mentors following mentor orientation and prior to the initiation of mentoring?
   C. Is there a plan for long-term mentor training?
   D. Are human resources identified to coordinate and implement each planned mentor training activity?
   E. Are material resources identified that are necessary to carry out mentor training?

VI. Mentor assignment and training
    A. Are there criteria established for assigning mentors?
    B. Is there a description of the procedures for matching mentors and protégés?
    C. Are criteria and procedures for matching mentors and protégés compatible with the overall purpose of teacher professional development for the district?

VII. System roles and responsibilities and mentor support
    A. Are program responsibilities at the district's central office, the building level, and other organizations clearly defined?
    B. Are the roles and responsibilities of all people who are involved in the mentor program clearly defined?

VIII. Rewards and mentors
    A. Are there extrinsic rewards for mentors (such as financial rewards or additional release time)?
    B. Are there provisions for school district recognition of particularly effective mentors?
    C. Are there incentives for mentors to engage in individualized activities in order to promote their personal and professional development?
    D. Are all elements of the plan for providing support and rewards for mentors compatible with your district's professional development program?
    E. Are human and material resources identified in order to coordinate support and rewards for mentors?

IX. Identifying appropriate target groups
    A. Will your mentoring program be directed exclusively at the needs of beginning teachers in your district? Or will it be available to all teachers?
    B. Is there a clear understanding of the kinds of issues that need to be included in mentoring programs for beginning teachers (as opposed to topics that are more appropriate for veterans)?

APPRAISAL: HOW DID IT WORK?

Finally, the mentoring planning team needs to consider a variety of questions that are designed to help determine whether the mentoring program achieved its goals and objectives, whether the implementation process seemed to be successful, and whether changes might be needed for the initial program design or implementation plan.

X. Program evaluation and revision
    A. Phases of program evaluation
        1. Context evaluation: Is there a plan for identifying environmental factors that might affect your mentoring program or its outcomes?

2. Process evaluation: Are there provisions for determining whether the mentoring program has been implemented according to your stated program goals?

3. Outcomes evaluation: Is there a plan to measure whether or not the program objectives have been met?

    B. Are there provisions for revising the mentoring program in response to the evaluation?

XI. Needs assessment for program modifications

    A. Mentors: Are provisions made for formal and informal ongoing needs assessments?

    B. Are human and material resources identified in order to coordinate and implement mentor needs assessment and corresponding modifications in the mentoring program?

SUMMARIZING THE CHAPTER

These questions are meant to help you as you begin to formulate a local approach to an effective teacher-mentoring program that can be used to assist with the professional development of teachers in your district. Simply responding to the questions, however, will not create your plan. Instead, you must look at your own local district's priorities and conditions in order to determine appropriate strategies to be used in developing an effective program.

In addition to the other issues that are raised in this chapter, it would be helpful to think of the following conditions that need to be addressed as part of the implementation process for a mentoring program in any district:

- Commitment on the part of the central office and the school board is critical.
- School board policy that is supportive of the program is important.
- A local mentoring planning team should be created.
- A budget must be planned.
- Requisite human and other resource materials need to be identified.
- The program structure should be designed.
- Goals and objectives are necessary.
- The implementation plan should be specified.
- Evaluation processes need to be identified before the program actually gets under way.

What Is Our Purpose? 3

This chapter considers some of the possible goals, objectives, and purposes that you might prepare as you set up the framework for the implementation of your local mentoring program for teachers. Again, you must take sufficient time to decide precisely why you want to have mentoring in your school system and which philosophy will guide your actions.

DECIDE THE TARGET GROUPS

Structured mentoring programs can be used to serve as part of the professional development process for two main groups of teachers: beginners and veterans. When planning your program, you need to decide early who will be the target of your effort. No matter which local vision or definition of mentoring you adopt, what will serve as the foundation for any mentoring program is the fact that this activity needs to be understood as part of a true developmental relationship that is tied to an appreciation of life and career stages. Unfortunately, most discussions of mentoring in education have not taken this perspective. The term *mentor* has traditionally been defined as anyone who is able to demonstrate craft knowledge to a beginner.

The assumption that you need to make when designing an effective mentoring program for teachers is that the role of the mentor will be different depending on the level of professional experience of the teachers. In other words, mentoring for beginning teachers is not the same as mentoring for experienced teachers. Mentoring for those who have just stepped into the classroom is different from the kind of support that is called for by teachers with ten, fifteen, or twenty years of experience. Most important, mentoring implies a professional activity and commitment that goes well beyond simply being able to answer questions about "the way we do things around here." Mentoring is a demanding form of teaching.

As you plan for an effective mentoring program, consider the following possible different groups for whom your program may be defined:

- *Inexperienced, beginning teachers:* These are individuals who are taking their first jobs as classroom teachers. They may have come from traditional undergraduate teacher preparation programs at universities, or from nontraditional "alternative" teacher certification programs that are increasingly being developed as a response to the national teacher shortage crisis. The common fact is that these people have had no full-time experience, with the exception of a brief period of student teaching or some other form of internship.

• *Experienced teachers who are new to your district:* In many districts, there are a number of people who are hired as teachers who have previous experience as classroom teachers. Unfortunately, it is assumed that those who have taught elsewhere come ready to step in as teachers in a new district without any guidance or support. However, anyone who is new to an organization needs assistance when it comes to learning about local norms, policies, practices, and issues. As a result, a mentoring program for experienced teachers who are new to your district is a valuable activity.

• *Veterans:* These are teachers who have more than a few years of experience working in your school district. The typical assumption is that because they have been in the organization for a while, they need no special guidance or assistance to help them do their jobs. In fact, the public norms of many school systems indicate that any experienced teacher who admits that he or she needs help is somehow an ineffective teacher. A value often implied in schools across the nation is that a "good teacher" handles every problem and issue within the confines of the classroom, without "bothering others." Mentoring can be an important form of support for any teacher. A paradox can often be heard in discussions related to this group, however. Chapter 4 includes characteristics of effective mentors and shows that they have had successful prior experiences in their roles. As a result, mentors will be drawn from the ranks of experienced teachers. What this implies is that your district might wish to consider developing mentors to assist mentors. Such a vision suggests that mentoring must be understood as a practice that goes well beyond simply answering some questions about how to do the job from time to time.

What group(s) do you plan to serve with your mentoring program? What data do you consult in order to help you make your decision?

_____

_____

_____

_____

_____

TWO CASES

Michael Hawkins spent the past four years working toward a goal he had since he was in the eighth grade at a middle school. At that time, he was encouraged by three of his teachers to think about a career in teaching. Michael kept that advice with him. When he graduated from high school, he attended State University, where he majored in elementary education. He completed all requirements for his state certificate, applied for a job in the Rolling Meadows Local Schools, and now he was about to step into his "dream" world as a fifth-grade teacher.

Michael was very eager to get off to a successful start as a teacher. He came to school nearly a week before the district's official starting date for teachers. After all, he wanted to set up his classroom in a way that would appeal to his pupils on the first day of school. He also knew that simply getting a state certificate and a teaching contract did little to answer all the questions that he now had as a beginning teacher. He had a positive experience when he did his student teaching last year, but now he was on his own. No cooperating teacher or supervising university faculty member would be there when he began to have questions about what to do in the "real world."

In the same school district, another teacher, Amanda Weis, was also getting ready to start the school year. Amanda would be teaching math to seventh graders at Vista del Monte Middle School, the same assignment that she had for the past eleven years. Before Vista del Monte, she had worked for five years at Crenshaw Middle School. She was known to her colleagues as a very competent teacher who went into each class well prepared and focused on helping all of her students.

The only problem was that Amanda Weis no longer personally felt that she was the successful and caring teacher seen by the eyes of others. She confided in her closest friends that the "spark was gone." Amanda felt as if her teaching was mechanically as good as ever, but her commitment to the profession was on the decline.

In each of these cases, how would a mentoring program for teachers be helpful to the two teachers?

_____

_____

_____

_____

_____

_____

_____

IDENTIFYING A PURPOSE

In addition to selecting the target groups for your mentoring program, it is also critical to understand that there are multiple purposes toward which an effective mentoring program can be directed. It is important to identify the specific purposes for which your program will be developed; otherwise, the mentoring program that you design might consist of little more than finding a few experienced teachers to answer questions from time to time. That would be fatal to the long-term well-being of your program.

Basically, most school districts want mentoring programs for two reasons:

1. *Career advancement:* This focus involves mentoring that stresses the grasping of technical skills that individuals need so that they can get and keep a job.

2. *Psychosocial development:* This approach to mentoring stresses a holistic approach to adult learning and encourages individuals to grow professionally as well as personally.

Neither of these purposes is wrong or incomplete. It is perfectly reasonable to develop a mentoring system that focuses exclusively on promoting career advancement, for example. Most mentoring programs that are designed for use in private corporations tend to focus primarily on providing career advancement support for protégés. For example, great effort is put into helping employees discover the ways to survive in the company and to move up the corporate ladder.

In schools, the notion of helping people move up is not as relevant as it is in many corporations (where there are often many opportunities to advance in terms of prestige, position, and pay). Schools tend to be relatively flat organizations with only a few possible levels of achievement. Nevertheless, the concept of career advancement has a value in education— particularly if the focus is on helping people survive the first few years of professional service.

By contrast, most private corporation mentoring schemes pay little attention to psychosocial development as a focus and purpose. In the field of teacher development, this purpose becomes much more accepted and therefore seems more appropriate. The life of a teacher is often lonely, frustrating, and filled with self-doubts and interpersonal conflict. As a result, the need for someone to provide for the schoolteacher's psychological well-being is clear.

As you develop your mentoring program for the teachers in your district, what will be the primary focus of your program?

_____

_____

_____

_____

_____

_____

Beyond the purposes for mentoring programs identified here, it is important to note that many other purposes might be listed for teacher mentoring. For example, school systems are well aware that retaining good teachers is a serious problem across the country. Providing support through formal mentoring programs may be a way to convince beginners to stay in the profession. Second, all teachers feel the pressures of recently adopted "high stakes testing" and other approaches to accountability in schools. Having mentors available for support is a way to reduce such stress. Finally, an increasing number of states are mandating the implementation of mentoring programs in local school districts—at least for beginners.

CHECKING YOUR PLAN

Refer to the questions that you were asked in Chapter 2, "Initial Program Development," to help you design a plan for your mentoring program. Note that many of the individual items refer specifically to issues that are considered in this chapter. Use the following checklist to assist you with reviewing important basic planning issues, and modify your plan accordingly.

A. Is there a statement of purpose for your implementation plan?
_____ Yes _____ No

   1. Is it consistent with the school board's philosophy of education?
_____ Yes _____ No

   2. The school district's mission statement?
_____ Yes _____ No

B. Is the purpose compatible with the following:
   1. The school board's philosophy of education?
_____ Yes _____ No

   2. The district's mission statement?
_____ Yes _____ No

   3. The professional development plan for the district?
_____ Yes _____ No

C. Are the fundamental reasons for the adoption of a mentoring program stated?
_____ Yes _____ No

D. Does the rationale include statements of belief concerning areas that are relevant to mentoring as a form of support for teachers?
_____ Yes _____ No

   1. Does each statement have a rational basis?
_____ Yes _____ No

2. Are the statements of beliefs compatible with each other?
_____ Yes _____ No

E. Does the rationale include specific implications of stated beliefs for mentoring?
_____ Yes _____ No

1. Do the specific implications flow logically from the general beliefs?
_____ Yes _____ No

2. Are the implications compatible with each other?
_____ Yes _____ No

F. Is the rationale compatible with the following:
1. The school board's general philosophy of education or expected outcomes?
_____ Yes _____ No

2. The school district's mission statement?
_____ Yes _____ No

G. Are broad program goals written?
_____ Yes _____ No

H. Are the goals appropriate for the stated needs?
_____ Yes _____ No

I. Are specific objectives written for each goal?
_____ Yes _____ No

J. Are the goals and objectives compatible with the following:
1. Goals and objectives of the district's professional development program?
_____ Yes _____ No

2. The purpose and rationale of the mentoring program?
_____ Yes _____ No

K. Does the plan include provisions for revising, adding, or deleting program objectives as a result of needs assessments that are administered to mentors and all teachers?
_____ Yes _____ No

L. Does the plan include provisions for mentors and all other teachers to set individual objectives?
_____ Yes _____ No

SUMMARIZING THE CHAPTER

This chapter considered the importance of understanding the purpose of a mentoring program before you actually begin to implement it in your district. Emphasis was placed on the following points:

- Mentoring programs can be designed for beginning or veteran teachers. You must decide which group is your focus or whether you wish to serve both groups.
- Mentoring programs can focus on career development, psychosocial development, or both objectives.

4 Who Is a Mentor?

Once the mentoring program planning team has considered the basic structure of your program, it is important to proceed with the implementation process. The most critical task involves determining what the mentoring program in your district should look like. This determination will automatically lead you to making a decision about another important issue; namely, who your mentors will be and what their specific responsibilities will be in meeting the challenges of your local program's definition.

In this chapter, you will find (a) information to help you decide who should and should not serve as mentors, (b) information about how to identify the ideal characteristics of mentors, and (c) information about a number of responsibilities for those who will be selected to serve as mentors to other teachers.

CHARACTERISTICS OF MENTORS: ONE CASE

Lori Duran has been teaching in the Longfellow City School District for eighteen years. She has been perceived as one of the strongest and most effective teachers in the system for several years. Two years ago, she was named the state Elementary School Teacher of the Year. When the mentoring planning team for Longfellow City was trying to identify good teachers to serve as mentors for the new teachers in the school district, Lori was at the top of everybody's list. Surely a teacher with her skill was exactly the kind of individual to serve as a role model and mentor for the newcomers in the district.

During the following school year, the mentoring program for new teachers in Longfellow City was started. Lori was assigned to work with her first protégé, Roger Carmichael—a bright young man who had just joined the faculty at Lori's school. He had graduated from Mount Charles College in the spring, and it was clear that he looked forward to his first teaching position with a lot of excitement and a bit of fear and caution as well.

At first, the relationship between Lori and Roger seemed to be very positive. They had weekly meetings concerning the kinds of things that often troubled beginning teachers (classroom management, lesson planning, parent conferencing, etc.). After about six weeks, however, the partnership between Lori and Roger seemed to change drastically. Roger was frustrated because Lori was always so busy with her own duties and commitments to the district teachers' association. She was rarely able to visit with Roger or respond to his questions. The other difficulty that was making Roger uncomfortable was the way Lori responded to his questions when he could make contact with her. She seemed to do little more than respond to his concerns by simply saying, "If I were you, I'd . . ." On more than a few occasions, Roger felt as if Lori were giving him answers only so he would not bother her any more.

Lori continued to enjoy being called a mentor teacher. She knew that Roger was making a few mistakes here and there, but they did not seem to be very drastic or serious. She felt as if she could always make the right calls and fix Roger's errors before they became too serious.

After reading this case study, would you consider Lori to be an effective mentor teacher? Why or why not?

What are some of the positive characteristics that would contribute to Lori's ability to serve as an effective mentor?

_____

_____

_____

_____

_____

_____

What are some of the negative characteristics that would suggest that she would be a poor selection as a mentor in the future?

_____

_____

_____

_____

If Lori has been identified as a mentor with some problems, what could the mentoring team suggest to her as ways in which she could improve her performance in the future?

_____

_____

_____

_____

CHARACTERISTICS OF MENTORS: A SECOND CASE

Calvin Hundley just finished signing his first contract as a high school English teacher. As the first person in his family ever to receive a college degree, he was very proud of his accomplishment. He looked forward to going back to Jefferson High School in Graniteville, his alma mater, so he could begin to repay his community with service as a dedicated and caring teacher.

One reason for Calvin's good spirits was that he was confident of his ability to serve as a good teacher from the start. The Graniteville City Schools had also started a new mentoring program where experienced teachers would be available to help first-year teachers negotiate some of the "rough spots." Just before the new school year started, Calvin received word that his mentor would be Lionel Baldridge, one of Calvin's former teachers at Jefferson. Lionel was acknowledged as being one of the best English teachers in the district, and clearly one of the teachers who had inspired Calvin to go into teaching in the first place. During the first weeks of the school year, Lionel and Calvin got together nearly every day for at least a few minutes to review some of the "tricks of the trade" that had enabled the mentor to enjoy a very successful career. Lionel was very careful not to tell Calvin "all that he needed to know." Instead, the protégé was invited simply to talk about his successes and challenges for the day, and Lionel avoided any temptations to "fix" Calvin.

After the first few days of the year, Lionel took on a very different approach. Now, he would interact with Calvin a bit less frequently, and when he did, he would simply listen to Calvin. After a few such sessions, Calvin and Lionel worked out a schedule of visits to each other's classrooms.

Calvin felt truly ready to take on the challenge of teaching. A big part of that feeling of readiness came about because of his mentor.

After reading this scenario, do you believe that Lionel is serving as an effective mentor? Why or why not?

What are some of Lionel's positive characteristics?

_____

_____

_____

_____

_____

Do you now have some teachers who are currently ready to step in and serve as mentors (as Lionel has done for Calvin)?

_____

_____

_____

ARE GOOD TEACHERS ALWAYS GOOD MENTORS?

Good mentor teachers must also be good teachers in the first place. However, the reverse is not true. Simply being a good teacher does not ensure that a person would be a good mentor. Being an effective mentor requires a variety of skills and abilities that often go beyond those required of a good classroom instructor.

Good teachers can be effective and help their colleagues in a school in a number of different ways:

- *As peer pals:* Individuals who are at the same level as their colleagues can share job-related information, strategies, and support for mutual benefit.
- *As career guides:* People who are not necessarily in positions in which they can champion or protect their colleagues but who can explain a system to others.
- *As sponsors:* Individuals who do not necessarily have organizational power but who can still promote and shape their colleagues' careers.
- *As patrons:* Influential people who can use their power to help advance other people's careers.

All of these roles are important. None is the same as being a true mentor, however—an individual who assumes the role of both teacher and advocate as part of an intensive, continuing, and mutually enhancing relationship. Mentors can engage in the same helping behaviors as peer pals, career guides, and so forth. But they go beyond these roles, and demonstrate characteristics that are even more focused on the needs of individuals with whom they are working.

Think back on your own career and reflect on people who served in the capacity of each of the roles that were listed here:

Peer Pal

_____

_____

Career Guide

_____

_____

Sponsor

_____

_____

Patron

_____

_____

Now consider one or more people whom you have known who were
more like the definition of a true mentor. List a few of these individuals
with whom you have had contact during your professional life and write
down some of the characteristics that they demonstrated to you to make
them effective mentors in your eyes.

_____

_____

_____

_____

WHAT ARE SOME CHARACTERISTICS OF EFFECTIVE MENTORS?

A number of desirable characteristics are listed here to aid you in selecting
mentors for teachers in your district:

1. Mentors should have experience as classroom teachers, and their
   peers and others should generally regard them as effective in the
   classroom.

2. Mentors need to ask the right questions of protégés. They do not
   merely provide the "right" answers all the time.

3. Mentors must accept an alternative way of doing things and avoid
   the temptation to tell protégés that the way to do something is "the
   way I've always done it."

4. Mentors should express the desire to see people go beyond their
   present levels of performance, even if it might mean that the protégés
   are able to do some things better than their mentors can.

5. Mentors need to model principles of continuous learning and reflec-
   tion on their practice.

6. Mentors must exhibit the awareness of the political and social realities of life in at least one school system; they must know the "real
   ways" in which things get accomplished.

Compare this list with the characteristics of mentors you have known.
Add any additional skills that you included in your review:

_____

_____

_____

In addition to these characteristics, other skills and abilities are often used to describe ideal mentors. Typically, these individuals demonstrate the following:

- Knowledge, skills, and expertise in a particular field of practice.
- Enthusiasm that is sincere and convincing—and, most important, the ability to convey this feeling to those whom they are mentoring.
- The ability to communicate to others a clear picture of personal attitudes, values, and ethical standards.
- The ability to communicate in a sensitive way the type of feedback that is needed regarding another person's progress toward desirable goals, standards, competence, and professional behavior.
- The ability to listen to colleagues' ideas, doubts, concerns, and questions.
- A caring attitude and a belief in their colleagues' potential, flexibility, and sense of humor.

These criteria are helpful in the selection process. Before selection, however, you must recruit individuals to become involved with your mentoring program. Five important skills must be shown by those who are to serve in a teacher-mentoring program:

1. They must have a willingness to invest time and energy in the professional development of their colleagues.

2. They must have a strong conviction and believe that other teachers are likely to have a positive effect on the quality of schooling.

3. They must have confidence in their own abilities.

4. They must possess high standards and expectations of their own abilities and the work of their colleagues.

5. They must believe that mentoring is a mutually enhancing professional development opportunity in which both partners will achieve satisfaction from the relationship.

DANGER SIGNALS

The following characteristics signal individuals who should probably not serve as mentors to teachers:

1. People who are too heavily involved with the internal politics of a school or district will generally be ineffective mentors. Often, their primary goals are simply to survive or to enhance their personal status in the system. (It is important for new teachers to develop insights into the political realities of their new world. It is not important for a novice teacher to learn how to spend a lot of time jockeying for a position or promoting specific agendas.)

2.   An individual must be comfortable in his or her position to serve as an effective mentor. (It might be wise, for example, not to invite a teacher who is new to a particular school or grade level to serve as someone else's mentor. The experienced teacher is likely to be going through a process of learning about a new system and will not have adequate commitment to the mentoring process.)

3.   A marginally effective teacher should not be selected to serve as a mentor on the basis that such an assignment would serve to "fix" his or her shortcomings. (Although it is true that service as a mentor can increase a teacher's effectiveness, it does not make good sense to match a beginner with anyone who is not able to demonstrate the very best behavior that is associated with an effective teacher.)

4.   Ineffective mentors demonstrate know-it-all behaviors and attitudes when discussing their approaches to teaching. Clearly, self-confidence is desirable in a mentor. Being closed minded about alternative teaching strategies or solutions for complex classroom problems, however, is probably a mark of a person's insecurity. It is hard to mentor others from such a perspective.

RESPONSIBILITIES OF MENTORS

Now that you have reviewed some of the characteristics of effective and ineffective teacher mentors, let's look at some of their major duties and responsibilities:

- To give their time to others
- To listen and sympathize with colleagues without necessarily condoning or condemning what might at times seem to be inappropriate or ineffective actions
- To manifest a sense of humor but to avoid sarcasm and cynicism
- To appreciate that good teachers are sometimes not able to play the role of effective teacher mentor, but that effective teacher mentors must always be good teachers

Another way of viewing the functions and duties of mentors is as follows:

- *Advising:* The mentor responds to a colleague's need to gain information that is needed to carry out a job effectively.
- *Communicating:* The mentor works to ensure that open lines of communication are always available.
- *Counseling:* The mentor provides needed emotional support to a colleague.
- *Guiding:* The mentor works to acquaint a new colleague with the informal and formal norms of a particular system.
- *Modeling:* The mentor serves as a role model by consistently demonstrating professional and competent performance on the job.

- *Protecting:* When needed, the mentor serves as a buffer between a colleague and those in the system who might wish to detract from that person's performance.
- *Skill Developing:* The mentor assists others with learning skills that they need to carry out their jobs effectively.

CHECKING YOUR PLAN

Check to see how well you have addressed each of the following items that deal with mentor recruitment and selection:

   A. Are eligibility requirements for becoming a mentor stated?

         _____ Yes _____ No

   B. Are procedures for nominating and selecting mentors stated?

         _____ Yes _____ No

   C. Are all elements of the mentor selection process compatible with the goals and objectives of the mentoring program?

         _____ Yes _____ No

SUMMARIZING THE CHAPTER

There are no magic recipes to ensure that everyone who is designated as a mentor will be effective in that role. In fact, there is likely to be no single person who will always be a perfect mentor to anyone at all times. After all, challenges face teachers at different times and under different circumstances. Multiple mentors are likely throughout a person's career. And it takes more than a long record of accomplishment as a recognized effective teacher to make someone a good mentor. It is a spirit that comes from within special people.

5 Preparing People to Serve as Mentors

There are those who say that the ability to serve as a mentor is a special gift. As a result, the whole notion of trying to prepare individuals to mentor others is impossible, they would say. You either have the talent or you do not.

Mentoring is indeed a talent. But it is also a special skill that even people with great insights and caring attitudes may not be able to demonstrate. As a result, training people for the role of mentors serving teachers is a critical aspect of any effective program. It is simply not effective to identify people as mentors and then throw them into service in that capacity. Focused learning activities will assist people become more effective mentors to their colleague teachers.

This chapter describes a model that can be used to prepare individuals as mentors in programs that are designed to support classroom teachers. There are five domains in the model, and for each domain, specific training activities are described.

DOMAIN 1: ORIENTATION TO MENTORING

Here, the primary goal is to develop a consensus definition of what mentoring is, what some of its benefits are, some problems that are traditionally associated with mentoring programs, and so forth. Devoting time to a general orientation for teachers of what mentoring is (and what it is not) is worthwhile for many reasons. First, the word *mentoring* has been so widely used to denote such a wide array of relationships that it has started to lose much of its real value. People frequently talk about mentors they have had, only to reveal that these mentors range from people who were available to "show new folks around" to the kinds of very thoughtful individuals who engage in mutually enhancing relationships, as they are promoted throughout this book. Finding a common definition of mentoring is an important first step in this vision of professional development for teachers.

It is often easier to identify true mentorship by identifying real-life examples from the lives of participants. If you were to identify people in your personal and professional life who have made a difference by helping you become the best that you can be, who would they be? (List the names of mentors whom you have had in the past.)

Based on your recollection of what these various individuals did to help you, what might your personal definition of mentoring be?

Discussions during training sessions can include many examples of real mentoring that have occurred in the lives of successful teachers. People talk frequently about a particular teacher from their high school days, a pastor, a spouse, or any one of hundreds of others who were influential in their lives. All of these stories are important in helping people appreciate the concept and value of mentoring.

DOMAIN 2: EFFECTIVE PLANNING AND MANAGING OF INSTRUCTION

The next part of training for mentors involves a consideration of the question, "Mentoring for what?" This question deals with the important issue of helping people decide what the outcomes of a mentoring relationship should look like. It is important to decide what benefits might be derived by a local school system if it invests time and money in a mentoring program. Will teachers who have mentors really become more effective?

In the following space, indicate some of the key characteristics that you believe should be displayed by effective teachers, as related to the effective planning and management of instruction and classroom practice:

Based on your experience as an educator, list some of the areas of instructional planning and management where you have noted problems on the part of classroom teachers, either as beginners or as veterans:

_____

_____

_____

Another important issue to be included in this part of the training involves the sharing of personal values, visions, and philosophies of the mentors and the teachers with whom they are working. Effective performance as a teacher is based in large measure on a person's ability to articulate clear and consistent personal values and beliefs. Consider, for example, the fact that teachers with clear expectations and beliefs related to student performance generally find that their students achieve at higher levels. Also, classroom management tends to be more effective in situations where teachers have communicated their expectations clearly to students.

Discussing personal philosophies held by both mentors and protégés might seem like a tedious activity, but it need not be. As people articulate their values and visions, open and meaningful dialogue becomes much easier to achieve. It is suggested, therefore, that part of the time that is spent looking at instructional practice should be devoted to helping people express fundamental values related to education. Some of the questions that are suggested to help people articulate their educational philosophies (or platforms) are as follows:

1. What do you hope to achieve in your teaching this year? How will you personally know if these goals are achieved?

2. How will students look after going through the next year in your class?

3. What will be your role in achieving these goals? What will be the role of your students and their parents or guardians?

4. What are some of the most important values you possess that cannot be violated? (What are the kinds of values that you hold before you start looking for another job?)

What are some additional questions that you believe would draw out an individual's personal core values and beliefs?

_____

_____

_____

Developing a personal philosophy or platform statement is a valuable activity. Sharing it with a mentor or protégé is even more powerful. This process can enable mentors to identify particular strengths of the protégés.

In turn, this situation enables people to celebrate success—an activity that is rarely done frequently enough in most organizations.

DOMAIN 3:
HUMAN RELATIONS SKILLS

The process of mentoring requires considerable skill in the area of effective human relations. Again, training in this area does not pretend to make people who have no great interpersonal skill become perfect overnight. Training here can identify some areas in which people need greater awareness of key ideas if they are to work effectively in the highly personalized world of effective mentoring, however.

Specifically, some information might be provided concerning adult learning and development and the importance of appreciating alternative learning or behavioral styles. For the most part, people who serve as mentors to other teachers are teachers. Therefore, they usually have considerable experience working with children as learners, but they have had little training and appreciation for the unique learning needs of adults. Furthermore, because people display a wide array of alternative behavioral and learning styles, it is critical for those who would serve as effective mentors to appreciate this diversity by understanding alternative styles.

To illustrate the kinds of things that differentiate the learning patterns of adults, take a moment to respond to the following questions about the last time that you, as an adult, learned something. (It does not need to be some major learning event, like learning the theory of relativity. It can be something as mundane as learning how to change the oil in your motorcycle, or learning a song on the piano, or how to use some new piece of computer software.)

1. Why did you want to learn it?

_____

_____

_____

2. To what old knowledge did the new learning connect?

_____

_____

_____

3. What is the current status of the new learning? What have you done with what you learned?

_____

_____

_____

Your answers to these questions will likely parallel many of the following characteristics of effective adult learning that have been identified by researchers over the years.

Adults learn best when:

1. The learning activities in which they engage are viewed as realistic and are of personal importance to the learner.

2. What is to be learned is viewed as related to some personal and/or professional goals.

3. The learner can receive accurate feedback about personal progress toward the goals.

4. The learner experiences success.

5. The motivation to learn truly comes from within the individual learner.

In contrast, it is also known that adult learners often resist experiences when

6. They feel as if the learning process has been an attack on their personal and professional competence.

7. They perceive that they are being provided prescriptions for learning that oversimplify complex issues.

These concepts are introduced into mentor training because of the importance of mentors' keeping a consistent image in their minds of the protégé as a colleague and also as an adult learner.

There are a number of different ways in which the concept of alternative behavioral patterns and learning styles might be introduced into mentor training. Many educators have gone through one or more of these exercises over the years. If you have, indicate some of the attributes that have been assigned to you:

_____

_____

_____

Regardless of the particular exercise that might be used in this part of the mentor training program, the activity is essential. The following assumptions are made relative to understanding and appreciating alternative styles:

1. People behave according to different behavioral styles. This occurs because people differ in how they perceive situations, work at tasks, interact with others, and make decisions.

2. People behave differently depending on the circumstances. In short, behavior changes.

3. There is no single "right" way for people to behave, but most people have an operating style that is most common and comfortable to them.

4. What feels comfortable and "right" for one person might feel uncomfortable and "wrong" to another.

5. An organization functions best when it capitalizes on the strengths of each individual and encourages the celebration of differences.

DOMAIN 4: MENTOR PROCESS SKILLS

In this part of the training, the major skills that are needed to carry out actual mentoring relationships are identified and described. These are the three major skill areas that are normally addressed:

1. Problem-solving skills

2. Listening skills

3. Observing skills

A major part of a mentor teacher's duties involve helping protégés— whether beginning or experienced teachers—resolve problems that they encounter while working in their classrooms or in other settings in their schools. As a result, training needs to include information to assist teacher mentors' work with others in identifying and ultimately solving problems encountered in their professional lives.

The following seven steps may be used to assist mentors or protégés analyze problems that they face on the job.

1. *Seek information about the problem in question:* If the existence of a particular problem is verified, this information can be useful for subsequent steps in the process.

2. *Define the problem:* Identify the desired situation and compare it to the actual one. Moving from the ideal to the desired situation is the goal of problem solving.

3. *Propose alternative strategies:* To solve the problem, generate as many potential strategies as possible. Hold evaluations of the feasibility of these solutions until later in the process.

4. *Select the strategies that will actually be implemented:* Weigh the advantages and disadvantages of each proposed alternative strategy.

5. *Design an implementation plan:* Translate your alternative strategies into specific actions; agree who will be responsible for doing what tasks; identify and secure needed resources; and plan to assess the value of the actions that were actually taken.

6. *Implement the plan.*

7. *Assess the implementation/action plan:* Did the action plan produce the desired situation that was identified in the first step of this process? Continue, modify, or abandon the action plan depending on the outcomes of the assessment.

Mentors might review these seven basic steps so they are ready to help the first-year teachers with whom they are working when the new teachers encounter problems that might call for this type of linear problem-solving model. Another effective technique involves examining and reviewing these steps as teacher protégés are asked to work through the particular problems and issues that they face on the job.

With regard to conferencing skills, much of the interaction between mentors and protégés takes place during one-to-one situations. Some information in the general literature that is related to peer coaching might be helpful to mentors who are seeking appropriate ways to work with protégés. Mentors need to adapt information that is presented in the literature in order to address the needs, concerns, and sensitivities that are found in mentor-protégé conferences.

The purpose of conferencing between teachers might be to address one or more of the following objectives:

1. Promoting the sharing of experiences and gaining support from a colleague

2. Promoting open communication

3. Sharing problems, generating alternative solutions, and selecting appropriate and feasible alternatives

4. Assisting mentors and protégés regarding particular problems

5. Providing assistance and encouragement

6. Providing for a supportive work environment so that both mentors and protégés can feel they are achieving professional growth and learning

In concrete terms, this part of the training strongly suggests that the conferencing between mentors and protégés should be based on periodic observations of each other's work in schools. After these observations take place, some of the questions that might be addressed by mentors and protégés include the following:

1. What did you see when you watched the other teacher?

2. What did you infer from his or her behavior?

3. What insights did you gain into your own behavior after observing the behavior of the other teacher?

4. How would you change your own behavior after what you have seen?

5. In what ways do you believe you are a more effective teacher after viewing the behavior of a colleague?

What might be some additional questions to consider after you have had the opportunity to discuss your interaction and observations of a colleague in your school?

_____

_____

_____

Finally, with regard to the process of identifying the observation skills that are needed by individuals who are serving as mentors to teachers, the important point to emphasize is that observation in this context is not a form of evaluation of teaching practice and performance.

DOMAIN 5: LOCAL IMPLEMENTATION ISSUES

Although the domains that are included in the training described here attempt to deal with as many as possible of the issues that will be encountered by mentors, it is also important to note that attention must be paid to the nature of local conditions and issues that exist in different states, schools, and districts. Time must be devoted to an examination of those local issues so that your mentoring program will fit into existing practices and programs. If it does not, it will likely be seen as just one more add-on responsibility to fill up the already busy lives of teachers.

The following topics are among the many that need to be considered at the local school district level as a district moves toward the adoption of a teacher-mentoring program.

1. Is there a commitment by the central office and school board?

2. Does mentoring fit with local board policy?

3. Who will be involved in planning the program?

4. How will individual needs be assessed?

5. How will a budget be handled?

6. What will our local program look like? What will be our structure?

7. What are our goals and objectives?

8. How will we know that our program goals and objectives have been met?

What additional questions do you believe you will need to consider in your own school system?

_____

_____

_____

_____

CHECKING YOUR PLAN

In Chapter 2, some issues were presented that might be included in a comprehensive plan to help you establish a local mentoring program. Return to that outline and see how far you have progressed in the section dealing with mentor training.

A. Is orientation planned for the mentors?

_____ Yes _____ No

1. Are goals and objectives for mentor orientation listed?

_____ Yes _____ No

2. Is there a tentative schedule of activities for mentor orientation?

_____ Yes _____ No

3. Does the plan for mentor orientation include making mentors aware of the following:
   a. Their roles and responsibilities?

   _____ Yes _____ No

   b. Mentor training activities in which they will participate?

   _____ Yes _____ No

   c. Your district's procedures for evaluating mentor performance?

   _____ Yes _____ No

B. Is there a plan to have preliminary training for new mentors following the mentor orientation and prior to the initiation of mentoring?

_____ Yes _____ No

1. Are the goals and objectives for preliminary mentor training listed?

_____ Yes _____ No

2. Is there a schedule of activities for preliminary mentor training?

_____ Yes _____ No

3. Do goals, objectives, and activities in the preliminary mentor training plan focus on knowledge and skills that

will be needed by mentors during the first few weeks of mentoring?

_____ Yes _____ No

C. Is there a plan for long-term mentor training?

_____ Yes _____ No

D. Are there plans for mentor orientation, preliminary training for new mentors, and long-term mentor training based on the development of a preliminary needs assessment?

_____ Yes _____ No

E. Are all elements of the plan for mentor training consistent with the purpose of the overall program of professional development in your district?

_____ Yes _____ No

F. Are human and material resources identified to coordinate and implement each planned mentor training activity?

_____ Yes _____ No

SUMMARIZING THE CHAPTER

This chapter presented a plan for training individuals to serve as mentors to their teaching colleagues. Three purposes for this training were noted:

1. Participants need to be presented with the basic definition and understanding of mentoring as an effective approach to professional development.

2. Individuals need to gain insights into professional behaviors that are related to effective mentoring for teachers.

3. People need to learn and practice the skills that are associated with effective mentoring for teachers.

6 Matching Mentors and Protégés

Assuming that you have worked very deliberately at setting up your mentoring program and that you have spent a lot of time selecting and training your mentors, what could possibly go wrong with your program? Unfortunately, the answer to this question is "plenty" if you ignore the material presented in this chapter.

This chapter considers how to match mentors and protégés. This topic may sound like a relatively simple matter, but it is more difficult than most people assume. Putting the wrong people together as mentors and protégés can be an extremely serious problem—one that could cause all of your hard work in establishing the program to be wasted. This situation is very similar to a couple that spends a lot of time together during a wonderful courtship, then spends many blissful hours arranging a beautiful wedding. And finally spends enthusiastic and happy days together on a romantic honeymoon—only to discover that the marriage will not last because the original match was not very good. There are many cases in which mentoring relationships have ended in bitter and unhappy "divorce" proceedings because the original courtship ignored some important signals.

A CASE OF A BAD MATCH

Tyrone McDaniels was a first-year teacher who had really thrown himself into his first job. He had taken seven years to complete his undergraduate degree and finish the work required for his state teaching license. After all, he also had to hold down a full-time job to earn money for university tuition and fees. Becoming a teacher was a dream come true, and Tyrone was committed to making his experiences at Green Meadows Middle School a success.

Despite his excitement at achieving an important personal and professional goal, Tyrone was also aware of the fact that, as a rookie, he needed someone to help him with the many questions that seemed to come up every day on the job. Fortunately, his district had initiated a program to support beginning teachers, and part of that program involved experienced teachers serving as mentors to newcomers. Because Tyrone was a man who taught social studies, it was an easy matter for the principal to find what she thought was a good match. David Justin, a teacher with eleven years' experience as a history teacher at Green Meadows, was assigned to work with Tyrone.

From the beginning, however, it was clear that conflicts were going to arise between Tyrone and David. Tyrone had an outgoing personality, whereas David was reserved and shy and generally preferred to stay out of most social conversations. On the other hand, Tyrone was an optimist who wanted to see every experience as an opportunity to learn more about his new role.

David was often negative and quite cynical. He was tired of teaching, so he responded to most of Tyrone's questions with one- or two-word answers (usually followed by more criticism of the school principal, the superintendent, other teachers, or parents).

What had started out to be an exciting year in Tyrone's mind was now turning into a nightmare. He needed a mentor, but the one he had been given was anything but a positive role model, supporter, or confidant. In short, Tyrone was only halfway through the first year of his life as a teacher, but he was already thinking about looking at some career options outside of education.

How could the Green Meadows principal have identified a better mentor for Tyrone?

MENTOR MATCHING: SOME MYTHS

Some of the myths that are often associated with the matching of teachers with effective mentors are highlighted in the case of Tyrone McDaniels. For example, it is generally assumed that because Tyrone was a man, he needed a male mentor. Also, it is widely assumed that mentors must come from the same subject area or grade level in which their protégés work. Neither of these beliefs is supported in the research regarding the most appropriate ways of matching people in mentoring programs.

With regard to the first issue of matching genders for mentoring, men prefer to have men as mentors (and women prefer women), but there are no clear-cut suggestions that men necessarily make better mentors to male colleagues. Matching mentors with protégés should be based on more than gender. The same responses would be given in the case of providing mentor support to racial or ethnic minority representatives.

With regard to the second myth—that mentoring must be only within the same subject area or grade level—by such reasoning, social studies teachers can learn nothing from English teachers, and second-grade teachers cannot be helped through contact with fifth-grade teachers. Although it may be true that many technical issues associated with teaching primary grades may be different from higher grade levels, the foundations of teaching remain the same in all subjects and grades. Issues associated with effective parent conferencing, for example, are the same in any school. As a result, true mentoring can easily occur across different grade levels and subject departments.

Another common belief regarding mentoring relationships is that mentors must be older than their protégés. Such a view is probably derived from common sense, and it is certainly consistent with the image of the mentor as the wise and more experienced colleague who knows all the answers and who can provide "truth" to the "new kids." The primary role of the mentor is not to know all of the answers but rather to work with a protégé to develop common understandings and solutions to concerns, issues, and problems that might occur in practice. A person's age has little bearing on the ability to mentor. There are numerous examples of younger colleagues guiding and mentoring older colleagues. Furthermore, if this were not the case, it would not be possible to establish and support mentoring programs designed for all teachers in a district. Peer relationships in such settings are critical for success. There are no absolute and persistent findings to show that those mentors who are younger than their protégés are not able to serve as effective mentors.

Finally, there are many people who suggest that mentoring relationships must be built on the geographical proximity of mentors and protégés. In other words, if mentors and protégés are not able to be together on a regular basis, mentoring relationships will be ineffective. This is a particularly important issue to be considered and addressed in mentoring arrangements for teachers. Often, the success of teacher mentoring is dependent on the likelihood that the partners in the mentoring relationship can drop in whenever they have a question to pose to their colleague.

SO WHAT SHOULD YOU USE?

The answers to this question are about as diverse as the number of school districts that are likely to adopt mentoring programs in the future. One district might have special conditions and characteristics that make it necessary to match mentors and protégés by using criteria that are quite different from those used in another school system.

Regardless of local conditions, there are some issues that might serve as possible considerations of ways to bring pairs of teachers together for mutual support:

1. *Learning styles:* One way in which there can be some effective sharing between partners in mentoring teams is if they are brought together

based on learning styles. Concrete and sequential learners might be better when working with each other, for example. One of the instruments that is often suggested for this purpose is the *Adult Learning Style Inventory* developed by David Kolb. (Additional information concerning this resource is found in the "Suggested Readings" section at the end of this book.)

2. *Common philosophies/educational platforms:* The articulation of one's personal educational platform as a frequent activity is an excellent form of professional development. It is a way in which a person is able to indicate a variety of personal values and beliefs regarding significant educational issues. Part of the training for mentors should be devoted to the development of these personalized statements. These statements should be shared, and that sharing can serve as an excellent start for matching between mentors and protégés.

What other issues and factors might serve as the basis for matching the teachers who serve as mentors and protégés in your school district?

_____

_____

_____

SOME ADDITIONAL THOUGHTS

Matching mentors and protégés in a structured, sensible fashion is neither easy nor precise. It would be highly desirable to match every teacher with a mentor who possesses a sincere and deep desire to spend time working with a colleague. The fact is, however, that such commitments are not always available.

The ideal matching of mentors and protégés should always be based on an analysis of professional goals, interpersonal styles, and the learning needs of both parties. It is nearly impossible in the real world to engage in such perfect matching practices. Most mentoring relationships will likely be formed as marriages of convenience and not as the ideal, naturally developing partnerships that are so often presented in the literature on organizational practice. If individual awareness of (a) the values found in mentoring, (b) a regard for mutual respect and trust, and (c) a sense of openness and positive interaction are all present, however, then the mentor-protégé relationship has the potential to become quite strong.

No magic recipes exist to guide the matching of mentors and protégés, but discussions about the ways in which you plan to match people ought to consider issues such as the following:

1. *Cross-gender mentoring:* This is an issue that needs to be considered at the local level. Will it be possible for males to work effectively with female colleagues (or vice versa)? (Remember that there are often broader concerns raised in this regard. Mentors and protégés must often work

together for many hours to discuss issues. Is this fact likely to cause concerns or problems because of the potential appearance of impropriety when a man and a woman work "after hours" too much?)

2. *Mentoring across organization levels:* Can a principal or assistant principal serve as a mentor to teachers? Can high school teachers mentor middle school or elementary school teachers?

3. *Differences in ages:* Can younger but more experienced teachers serve as effective mentors to older colleagues who may now just be starting their careers in classrooms? Can they serve as mentors who have experience and are coming into your school system from another district?

At the local level, you must address the answers to these and many other similar questions that are related to strategies that can be used to match mentors with protégés. Local conditions such as (a) the personalities of mentor teachers and other educational leaders, (b) local norms and traditions of professional cooperation, and (c) other aspects of life in particular school systems are likely to have a major impact on the ways in which your program might be developed.

CHECKING YOUR PLAN

A. Are criteria established for assigning mentors to protégés?
_____ Yes _____ No

Are the criteria compatible with the knowledge base on matching mentors and protégés?
_____ Yes _____ No

Do the criteria reflect practical considerations of the program size, type, and numbers of potential mentors?
_____ Yes _____ No

B. Is there a description of the procedures for matching mentors and protégés?
_____ Yes _____ No

Do the procedures address the concerns of those directly affected by mentor assignment?
_____ Yes _____ No

Is the issue of mentor reassignment during the school year addressed?
_____ Yes _____ No

C. Are criteria and procedures for matching mentors and protégés compatible with the overall purposes of professional development in your school district?
_____ Yes _____ No

SUMMARIZING THE CHAPTER

This chapter addressed a number of issues dealing with bringing mentors and protégés together in some reasonable fashion. There are no perfect answers to how to bring people together for effective professional development relations.

Despite limitations on absolute, correct answers for mentor-protégé matching, however, this issue has a lot to do with the overall perceptions of the program's effectiveness. A good system should offer the kind of flexibility in which it is possible for individual teachers to identify and work with multiple mentors throughout their careers. After all, in mentoring, long-term bonding between two people is not always a virtue. At times, it may be the most ineffective approach to a positive and mutually enhancing relationship.

7 What Do Mentors Do?

This question has been asked more than a few times as new mentoring programs have been launched in school districts across the nation. The lack of response to this question is the single greatest cause of programs disappearing after they have been initiated.

People generally like the idea of starting a program of support for schoolteachers, whether the teachers are beginners or veterans. Mentoring is an appealing concept. Even when additional resources need to be found in order to initiate mentoring, this effort is not in itself a major inhibitor to the implementation and maintenance of a program.

The one obstacle that does not serve to discourage people to the extent that they ultimately decide to give up on mentoring is feeling as if they do not know what they are supposed to do in their assigned jobs. Research on adult learning and development consistently shows that (a) adults do not wish to feel as if they are incompetent—that they cannot do something to which they have been assigned; (b) people feel frustrated when they cannot master a skill, such as using a particular computer program; and (c) people sometimes feel inadequate to serve effectively as mentors for colleague teachers (no one wants to fail at an important task).

A CASE IN POINT

The Greenbriar School District, like many other school systems across the nation, was facing a severe challenge with the recruitment of many new teachers in the next few years. In fact, it was clear that they would need to hire nearly 200 new teachers for the next year alone. In order to retain those who would be hired, it was decided to initiate a new mentoring program designed primarily to help beginners get off to a good start. There was considerable enthusiasm in the district over the new program. Armando Flores was a teacher in the district for several years, and he was among several individuals who eagerly volunteered to go through some additional training to become prepared as a teacher mentor in his school. Although he now had nine years of experience "in the trenches," he could still recall his rookie year. As a result, he was glad to be a resource to help inexperienced colleagues in the future.

Armando was most pleased to hear that the old "sink or swim" notion of bringing new teachers into the schools was changing, and this mentoring program seemed to be a major commitment toward providing help. He attended the training sessions, developed a personal vision of what the value of mentoring would be, and now was looking forward to helping two new teachers who would be working in his school in the fall. As directed during the mentor training session, Armando had taken the initiative to schedule two meetings early in the school year with his protégés. These took place during the teacher workdays just before the first day of school. He spoke with both new teachers on the phone, and it was clear that they were both enthusiastic and apprehensive about their first days on the job. Armando wanted to help as much as possible.

In his coaching and mentoring the two new teachers, what are some key issues that you feel Armando should share with his protégés as they begin their new professional careers?

Issue 1

_____

_____

_____

Issue 2

_____

_____

_____

Issue 3

_____

_____

_____

There are a variety of essential skill areas in which a mentor can assist people when they assume a new role, or even help people who already have teaching experience become more effective. Some of these include the following:

Framing Issues. For an individual who is taking on a new teaching position, the job can be overwhelming—considering all of the issues that need to be addressed. The first thing that you need to do when you begin working with a protégé is to frame the broad issues that are to be considered. For example, your protégés may decide that they are very concerned about classroom management and student discipline (a good bet!). Although it may be easy to identify and frame a problem such as this, other issues may require a little more discussion.

It is critical that both the mentor and protégés (whether they are beginners or veterans) establish some basic rules about openness and honesty in their discussions. Some subjects (e.g., effective classroom management techniques) might become the objects of ongoing discussions, while some topics might be less enduring. For instance, how to work with parents at the first parent conference session of the school year might be addressed during one relatively brief conversation.

Identifying Goals. Once the mentor has worked with protégés in order to identify some of the broad issues that need to be addressed, it is possible to look at long-term as well as immediate personal and professional goals. In a positive working relationship between a mentor and a protégé, it is helpful for a mentor to guide and support the aspirations of the protégé. Although the mentor can help the protégé focus on long-term goals, a more immediate goal should be to address a particular concern at each mentoring session. Regardless of whether the mentoring is helping the protégé articulate long-term or immediate goals, you might find the following key ideas about goal setting to be valuable:

- Goals should be achievable and realistic
- They should be measurable in terms of quality, quantity, or time
- Ideally, they should be totally agreed upon by both the mentor and the protégé, but it is the protégé who should be responsible for initially proposing them

Promoting Self-Directed Learning. A big part of mentoring, particularly when working with new teachers, is to help protégés grow into their new roles. The key to a successful mentorship is the extent to which the protégé becomes comfortable with taking greater control over personal learning experiences. In short, the goal of good mentoring should be to make the protégé's reliance on the mentor eventually disappear.

There are a number of guidelines that you can follow to increase a protégé's self-directed learning:

- *Listen actively:* Let protégés explain their concerns, fears, hopes, goals, or anything else that might be on their minds. Avoid the temptation to step in with well-intentioned statements such as, "It sounds to me that what you are trying to say is . . ." Many mentors are tempted to intervene too quickly. It is important that the mentor begin the relationship by simply *listening* to the protégé.

- *Help protégés understand the consequences of their actions:* The worst thing that a mentor can do is to tell protégés that they should not do something because "I knew it wouldn't work." Instead, the mentor should try to assist the protégé to understand why something should (or should not) be done by asking, "What do you think might happen if you made that decision?"

- *Share experiences:* Let protégés understand that even the worst mistakes have been made before. No one, not even the wisest and most experienced mentor, has been a perfect teacher. "We all make mistakes" might be a very powerful observation to share.

- *Establish limits:* Protégés might become frustrated if they discover that mentors have not been completely open about the limitations of certain courses of action before they were taken. Although it may be desirable to encourage protégés to take risks and be creative, mentors should clearly state any restriction that might apply to a certain approach.

A mentor's job is to find the appropriate balance between supporting innovative and creative approaches to teaching on the part of protégés and remaining honest and candid about limitations.

Mentoring is a means of assisting and guiding the work of others. Mentors become increasingly effective as protégés decrease reliance. This situation is achieved through the mentor's willingness to empower the protégé. A mentor can do three things to build a sense of empowerment in protégés:

1. Encourage protégés to do most of the talking while making use of nondirective consultative skills.

2. Encourage protégés to move from the role of student to the role of teacher and become leaders of mentor-protégé relationships (appreciating the fact that protégés are not the only learners in effective mentoring relationships).

3. Remain open and honest with their protégés (they must be prepared to give the "straight scoop").

Empowering for action also implies that the mentor serve as a mediator within an organization. There are times when an experienced teacher in a school knows the right way to get things done (who to call, what forms to fill out, who to ignore, etc.).

Summarizing. An effective mentor must, in discussions with the protégé, summarize any agreements that are reached. This procedure ensures a complete understanding of what has been discussed and any plans that have been made.

It is far better for mentors to check for shared understanding while there is direct contact between themselves and protégés, rather than to try to fix the results of mixed communication later.

ADDITIONAL RESPONSIBILITIES OF MENTORS

In very general terms, mentors are able to work with individual protégés to help build the following:

- Feelings of personal and professional competence
- Self-confidence
- A greater sense of direction
- Increased professionalism

Mentors can also provide assistance to other teachers in at least five additional areas that are traditionally associated with effective performance by teachers:

1. Gaining knowledge of school district curriculum and available instructional resources.

2. Improving instructional skills and classroom management skills.

3. Serving as role models for completing teacher tasks.

4. Sharing effective strategies and practices for developing positive relations with parents.

5. Helping protégés formulate personalized insights into developing productive and satisfying classroom environments so that student learning can be improved.

What are some of the other responsibilities that you can identify for mentors in your district as they help colleagues become more effective teachers?

_____

_____

_____

_____

Consultation Skills

Mentor-protégé relationships are based on a number of fundamental skills that are used in consultation settings. The following are skills that effective mentors need to exhibit:

- Listening
- Sharing information
- Treating others with respect
- Facilitating team membership
- Developing informal relationships
- Giving feedback and being open to receive feedback

- Giving credit to others for their ideas
- Demonstrating a willingness to learn from others
- Recognizing and responding to individual differences

Return to the case study and assume that you are the mentor teacher. What if your protégés came to you with problems concerning their relationships with the building custodian who was not cooperating with requests to clean classrooms more completely each day? They note that their goal is to provide a safe and inviting learning environment for their students. However, they are not comfortable approaching the custodian, who does not appear to be very friendly. They do not want to develop a negative relationship with the custodial staff. How would you use the nine steps listed previously to work through the issue with your protégés?

Listen to Others

Share Information

Treat Others With Respect

Facilitate Team Membership

Develop Informal Relationships

Give Feedback and Be Open to Feedback

_____

_____

_____

Give Credit to Others for Their Ideas

_____

_____

_____

Demonstrate a Willingness to Learn From Others

_____

_____

_____

Recognize and Respond to Individual Differences

_____

_____

_____

DEVELOPING AN ACTION PLAN

An important part of forming an effective mentor-protégé relationship is to make certain that there is a high degree of clarity regarding the interactions that are expected to occur over time. As a result, a practical suggestion is that mentors and protégés should work out a clear action plan early in the school year. This action plan would involve the identification of priority goals, specific objectives, activities that assist the protégé with reaching the stated goals and objectives, and some way of identifying whether or not the goals and objectives have been achieved. Appendix B contains a mentor-protégé action planning form that might be helpful to you when carrying out this type of mentor-protégé planning.

CHECKING YOUR PLAN

Review your plan for mentor descriptions as developed in this chapter and compare it to the plan that you have established for implementation.

A. Are program responsibilities of your school district's central office, responsibilities at the building level, and responsibilities of other organizations (e.g., your local teacher association) involved in the mentor program clearly defined and delineated?

_____ Yes _____ No

B. Are the roles and responsibilities of all people involved in the mentoring program clearly defined?

_____ Yes _____ No

C. Supports and rewards
1. Are provisions made for regular group meetings that focus on support for mentors?

_____ Yes _____ No

2. Is a support person identified to coordinate the activities of mentors?

_____ Yes _____ No

3. Are mentors provided with sufficient time to carry out their responsibilities?

_____ Yes _____ No

4. Are provisions made for mentors to receive resources essential for carrying out their mentoring responsibilities?

_____ Yes _____ No

D. Rewards and mentors
1. Are there extrinsic rewards for mentors, such as financial rewards or additional release time?

_____ Yes _____ No

2. Are there provisions for school district recognition of particularly effective mentors?

_____ Yes _____ No

3. Are there incentives for mentors to engage in individualized activities to promote their personal and professional development?

_____ Yes _____ No

E. Are human and material resources identified to coordinate support and rewards for mentors?
1. The purpose of your district's professional development program?

_____ Yes _____ No

2. The rationale, goals, and objectives of your district's professional development program?

_____ Yes _____ No

SUMMARIZING THE CHAPTER

In this chapter, a number of ideas were presented to help you answer the important question, "Now that I'm a mentor, what do I do?" Mentor-protégé relationships are often viewed as most effective when (a) they are developed so that they demonstrate warmth and respect between the parties, and (b) when they serve as motivators for the mentor and protégé to grow professionally. Effective mentoring requires a commitment of time, energy, and effort. But all of this hard work pays off in terms of extremely positive outcomes for mentors, protégés, and school districts.

There are no magic answers to questions about specific mentoring activities. The simplest suggestions are often critical to successful relationship building, however. As a result, you might wish to consider the following suggestions as key ideas to include as you work with colleagues as protégés in the process:

- Smile and be pleasant
- Praise and celebrate your colleague's success
- Encourage your colleagues to be the best that they can be
- Always focus on strengths and not weaknesses
- Display confidence in the ability and judgment of your colleagues
- Support the mentoring relationship
- Help your colleagues realize present skills and abilities and then build on these assets

Mentoring for Beginning Teachers 8

A few years ago, there seemed to be a worldwide recognition that schools were facing a problem because fewer people wanted to serve as teachers. And one of the reasons given over the years for the waning interest in the field of teaching has been that people who go into this field are not provided much support, respect, or assistance. This is particularly true for those who are in the first few years of teaching. Traditionally, teachers have been treated as if they are wholly "replaceable parts" in a factory. It's as if a new teacher who came to a school to replace someone who retired after thirty years of service in a classroom was expected to fit in and do the same job as the veteran. Being "certified" (or "licensed") has traditionally been viewed as being "prepared" and ready to step into a classroom and immediately and competently fulfill all duties traditionally assigned to all other teachers.

At the same time, it is increasingly more evident that beginning teachers are becoming frustrated during their first few years in the classroom. This no doubt leads to the shocking fact that, for the past decade, the trend has been for new teachers to leave the field of education quickly. More than fifty percent of today's entering classroom teachers will leave the profession before they have five years of experience. One of the most frequently noted factors contributing to this situation is that beginners often become discouraged because they are expected to perform their teaching duties with the same skill and confidence as colleagues with many years of classroom experience. It is increasingly clear that specialized support for beginners is needed.

Fortunately, many school districts and states have recognized the importance of support programs for novice teachers. Induction programs have been developed across the nation as a way to assist those who are entering classrooms for the first time. A central ingredient in these beginning teacher programs has generally involved the adoption of some type of mentoring.

Mentoring can be a particularly effective process to help the beginning teacher. To emphasize this fact, consider what it was like when you first became a teacher. What are some of the questions and issues that you considered during your first week on the job?

_____

_____

_____

_____

_____

_____

_____

_____

_____

Now, list some of the ways in which a person who might have served in the role of an assigned mentor could have assisted you in dealing with any of these issues:

1. Issue:

_____

_____

_____

_____

My mentor could have helped me by

_____

_____

2. Issue:

_____

_____

_____

_____

My mentor could have helped me by

_____

_____

3. Issue:

_____

_____

_____

_____

My mentor could have helped me by

_____

_____

4. Issue:

_____

_____

_____

_____

My mentor could have helped me by

_____

_____

5. Issue:

_____

_____

_____

_____

My mentor could have helped me by

_____

_____

BEGINNING TEACHERS' NEEDS

Researchers looking into issues regularly report that major concerns of beginning teachers tend to fall into several predictable categories:

1. *Management Concerns:* Issues such as how to plan classes, manage student behavior, comply with school district rules and policies, and so forth.

2. *Personal Concerns:* Since many beginning teachers are starting their first full-time jobs after graduating from college, they are concerned with setting up their residences, establishing financial arrangements, paying off student loans, perhaps finding schools for their own children, and many similar tasks.

3. *Instructional Concerns:* Learning how to serve the needs of students enrolled in the new teacher's classes.

4. *Socialization Concerns:* What does it mean to be a "teacher"? What are the social realities of teaching?

Another framework describing the kinds of issues faced by beginning classroom teachers has been suggested by Esther Letven (1992, pp. 65-72). She noted that novice teachers are affected by the following sets of influences:

- *Personal Environmental Influences:* Beginning teachers are seeking to clarify their professional identities, and they are also frequently struggling with doubts about their personal professional competence.
- *Organizational Environmental Influences:* Beginning teachers go through a "culture shock" as their idealism often runs directly into and contradicts the realities of daily life in classrooms.
- *Professional Growth Needs:* Beginning teachers need to determine personal thinking and behavior patterns and see if these are appropriate for their new professional roles.

A CASE STUDY

Robin McCarthy had just graduated from Rockwell State University. With a strong major in mathematics and all the courses and student teaching required by Rockwell for secondary school teaching certification, she felt ready to move forward and step into a job she had dreamed about since she was in fourth grade. She was going to be a teacher!

Not surprisingly, she had several offers for teaching positions. She had strong grades throughout her undergraduate studies, excellent references, and with a major in math and a minor in chemistry, she was being sought by nearly every high school within a hundred miles of her home. After reviewing several offers, she finally decided to take a position at Mount Raymond High School in the Carson Creek Schools. Carson Creek not only offered her the highest starting salary, but also enjoyed a longstanding reputation as an excellent school system. More than 80 percent of students at Mount Raymond went on to college. When she went to the high school for her interview, she was impressed by the teachers on the staff, who seemed to be both friendly and quite professional. Mrs. d'Alessandro, the math department chair, was particularly helpful and open to questions. She also liked Mr. Stankowski, the principal, who appeared to be the kind of person who would be fair to a beginning teacher.

It was now a few days before Robin was to begin her first year as a teacher. She had made several trips to the high school during the summer as she brought in books, desk supplies, family photos, posters, and other similar items, and even a collection of "Inspirational Mottoes" to hang on her classroom walls as a way to assure all of her students that success in studying math was something they could all achieve. Now, she started to have some genuine anxiety attacks. Can she really do the job? Will the kids respect her? Will she look foolish in front of other teachers and administrators? All of these things were crossing her mind at the same time that she was wondering if her take-home pay would be enough to take care of her rent, utilities, groceries, and car payment. And would she be able to put aside a few dollars so that she could begin taking graduate courses next summer? That was a promise she made to the principal and the interview committee when she applied for this job. After all, Mount Raymond High School had very high standards. Every teacher with more than five years of experience on the staff had at least a master's degree.

On the one hand, Robin was truly very happy to be a teacher. On the other hand, could she really do the job? It sure would be good to be able to sit down and share these thoughts with somebody!

HOW COULD MENTORING HELP?

Review the lists of issues faced by beginning teachers that was presented just before the case study. What types of concerns or influences could you identify and use to describe Robin as she started her first year as a teacher?

_____

_____

_____

Describe the kinds of things that you would talk to Robin about if you were to serve as her mentor.

_____

_____

_____

If you were in charge of a teacher-mentoring program in Robin's school district, what skills would you expect of this first-year teacher's mentor so Robin would have a successful start in her new career?

_____

_____

_____

Robin McCarthy is a fairly typical beginning teacher. She is loaded with enthusiasm and high expectations for what her life will be like in the classroom. She will undoubtedly have days when her Inspirational Mottoes will seem like a bad idea, and there will be many times when she will realize that ninth graders in Algebra I and tenth graders enrolled in Geometry may not be as dedicated to the serious study of mathematics as Robin might have hoped.

Robin is also facing multiple types of doubts as she prepares for her first day in the classroom. She has doubts about her ability to fit in with more experienced staff. She wonders if she can project enough authority and expertise to control students and satisfy parents. Above all, she now has some doubts about her readiness to teach math: Is she truly competent?

Coupled with all of these concerns, she is also facing the issues that many young professionals do when they take their first jobs after completing college. Can she "hack it" out in the real world, on her own?

This brief case study shows an excellent example of a novice teacher who can profit from contact with an experienced teacher serving as her mentor. The topics that the mentor might talk about with Robin during the days before the school year begins include the following:

Lesson Planning. Has the new teacher developed strong enough lesson plans to carry her through the first several days of the new school year? It is critical to have an intended "game plan" so that there is a flow of teaching from day to day. The beginning will surely be hectic for the rookie, so having less need to do a lot of last minute planning each night before the next school day will make life a lot easier.

What other things might you do to help a protégé in developing an effective lesson plan for the start of the school year?

Familiarity With Surroundings. Does the new teacher know her way around the school building? Where are the copy machines? What about the counselors' offices? Where are the best parking places found for teachers? There are so many things happening in the life of a rookie teacher that not knowing the location of a telephone can be just one more frustration that may lead to a miserable beginning to a career.

If you were working with a first-year teacher, what are some of the places around your school that you would make sure to include in a tour?

Knowledge of Rules and Policies. What are some of the rules that a beginning teacher needs to know at the beginning of a school year? For example, what is the school policy on counting a student "tardy" as opposed to being "absent"? Is there a dress code for students? While a review of these kinds of things may not seem to be terribly exciting, learning about expectations for student behavior can be a true lifesaver for a beginning teacher. Imagine how embarrassing it would be for a conscientious first-year teacher if a group of eleventh or twelfth graders decided to begin the year by playing games with the new teacher. A mentor can help by reviewing the student handbook and noting some of the fairly typical violations that are likely to occur at the beginning of each school year.

What are some things that you would make certain to point out to a beginner in your school?

Review of Faculty Expectations and Operating Procedures. What do administrators and other teachers expect of a colleague? Again, the experienced teacher serving as a mentor can provide a great overview of things that must be done, and things that must not be done—both officially and according to the local norms and culture of a particular school.

What are some of these issues that you would share with an inexperienced colleague in your school?

_____

_____

Ask How the New Teacher is "Settling In" as a New Resident of the Community. As a new teacher, it is quite comforting to have someone ask you about your life outside of school. "Have you found a good supermarket yet?" can be an extremely important question to hear from a coworker. So can "If you need work done on your car, let me tell you a good place." While a mentor cannot solve a protégé's personal, financial, or domestic problems, it is always nice to know that someone actually cares about the person, not just the worker. Remember that a good deal of research on beginning teachers by Frances Fuller (1969) and Gene Hall and Susan Loucks (1978) has shown that novice teachers are likely to need more direction in terms of help with personal concerns before they are able to turn their attention to professional issues.

What are some of the issues that you would bring up to help a beginning teacher feel more personally secure?

_____

_____

List some of the additional topics and issues that you might raise with a beginning teacher prior to the beginning of a school year.

_____

_____

_____

Besides helping with these issues, mentors can be extremely helpful to beginning teachers by reviewing some of the following items that might be critical in dealing with problems that novices often face:

• *Personal educational platform for the beginning teacher:* What are some of the most important and central educational values of the new teacher? What are the non-negotiable values that the new teacher believes should not be violated by any demands of the new job?

• *Vision:* What does the new teacher hope to accomplish during the first year on the job? Besides simply surviving, what will be some of the indications that the newcomer might demonstrate as an affirmation of success during the first year?

• *Personal identity:* What will it feel like to have students, parents, other teachers and staff, and administrators look to the beginner as a professional educator and expert?

What are some of the other items of this nature that you believe should be covered before the school year begins?

_____

_____

_____

In the first few weeks after the school year has begun, the following might ordinarily deserve some conversations between mentors and beginning teachers:

- *Lesson development:* How to modify the lesson plans in light of actual student needs and performance
- *Classroom management:* Maintaining class control without becoming a tyrant
- *District policies and school procedures:* Continuing to enforce school and district policies in the classroom
- *Motivation:* Keeping the interests and focus and efforts of students alive as the school year begins to "drag on"
- *Interpersonal relationships:* Maintaining positive and productive working relationships with other teachers and staff members
- *Taking time for student needs:* Getting to know students as people, and providing honest and effective feedback
- *Housekeeping details:* Remembering not to miss important deadlines, maintaining accurate records and dates, getting students ready for statewide assessment tests, and so forth

Additional items to consider in your school or district might include the following:

_____

_____

_____

As the first school year progresses, the following topics might also be considered as part of the ongoing dialogue between the new teacher and his or her mentor:

- *Communication:* Maintain open communication with parents or other caregivers, both in terms of formal conferencing and through other approaches.
- *Classroom management:* This is a continuing concern of beginning teachers and deserves ongoing attention in conversations between mentors and protégés.
- *Focus on learning and teaching:* As beginners become more comfortable with their surroundings, it is nonetheless critical that intensity and focus is maintained on instruction and student learning.
- *Housekeeping, again:* It is important to stay on top of all important deadlines and the other housekeeping chores expected of teachers.

Other items that might be addressed throughout the school year in your district and school include the following:

_____

_____

_____

The items listed here tend to be associated with helping people become oriented to a new school or district, and they are important. Simply going over these matters is not all there is to a teacher-mentoring program, however. As noted previously, in the discussions of what occurs prior to the beginning of the school year, mentors and new teachers must have the opportunity to meet concerning socialization issues. These are things that will help a rookie teacher feel more comfortable for the first time.

When it comes to socialization, it is more difficult to assign specific issues that need to be addressed at different times during the school year. Instead, discussions along these lines are best handled on an ongoing basis and as new teachers come forward with concerns. Some of the issues that might be covered, however, during face-to-face conversations, include the following:

- *Platforms:* Again, discussions of personal educational platforms and philosophies represent dialogue concerning fundamental values. These always deserve attention.
- *Adjustment:* Ways in which students, teachers, and other staff seem to be adjusting to the new teacher. Also, ways in which the new teacher is adjusting to new people, duties, and places.
- *Personal issues:* How is the new teacher adjusting to the strains now placed on her or his personal life as a result of the new job and its time demands?
- *Self-evaluation:* How can you tell if you are really doing a good job?

Other issues that might be considered relative to how well a new teacher is fitting in are as follows:

_____

_____

_____

Finally, mentors can assist newly hired teachers in many other ways. Regardless of the competence and ability of people who were recently hired, it is not likely that they will possess all of the knowledge, skills, and insights that are expected of experienced teachers. As a result, discussions between new teachers and mentors might include the following:

- The prevailing technology expectations for all teachers and how to learn more if these skills are a problem
- The vision of effective teaching and learning and instruction that exists in a school

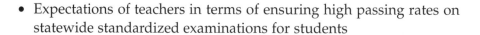

- Expectations of teachers in terms of ensuring high passing rates on statewide standardized examinations for students

Other similar issues that might warrant conversations between mentors and teachers in your school or district are as follows:

_____

_____

_____

SUMMARIZING THE CHAPTER

The information in this chapter was designed to help you with a mentoring program that is planned to help beginning classroom teachers in your school and district. Some issues that are discussed between mentors and newcomers are related to only specific systems or schools. However, there are many things that any new teacher in any school system might need to know. Some of these items were noted here.

REFERENCES

Fuller, Frances. (1969). Concerns of teachers: A developmental model. _Journal of Teacher Education, 76_(2), 207-226.

Hall, Gene, & Loucks, Susan. (1978). Teacher concerns as a basis for facilitating and personalizing staff development. _Teachers College Record, 80_(1), 36-53.

Letven, Esther. (1992). Induction. In Ralph Fessler & Judith Christensen (Eds.), _The teacher career cycle: Understanding and guiding the professional development of teachers._ Boston: Allyn & Bacon.

Mentoring for Veterans 9

Chapter 8 discussed the importance of developing mentoring programs that are geared toward helping beginning schoolteachers achieve initial success on the job. Such efforts are extremely important in promoting ongoing professional development for teachers. Mentoring is a practice that can be geared toward the needs of all teachers, however—regardless of experience.

This chapter presents some ideas that you can use to develop a mentoring program that will assist veteran teachers. As you may recall from Chapter 3, a primary (or even a sole) focus of your work might be on this important group of professionals. The material presented here will be helpful as you look for a way to meet their learning needs.

MENTORING FOR VETERANS: TWO CASES

Annette Grayson had been an elementary school teacher in the Forest Green Local Schools for nine years. Last year, her husband was transferred by his company to a new assignment in a city in the northern part of the state. Annette was able to find a job very quickly as a fifth grade teacher in Horizon Valley, a school system with an excellent reputation based largely on student performance each year on the State Achievement General Examination (SAGE). She also heard that parents in the district had very high expectations for student performance. That could present some frustration to teachers. But Annette was so happy to be able to land a job in such a well-respected school district that she decided not to be distracted by some potential problems that might or might not appear in the future.

From her first day on the new job in Horizon Valley, it was clear to Annette that life was going to be considerably different from what it had been in Forest Green. Teachers seemed to be much more sophisticated; there was no one in her school who had less than a master's degree and several years of experience. Forest Green had been a "revolving door" school district, where many teachers stopped in for only a year or two to get enough teaching experience to find better jobs in other districts in the state.

At Horizon Valley, Annette soon found out about parent involvement and high expectations. Mothers and fathers seemed to be walking around the school constantly, and she had many parents who stopped in to visit her class. Even though she found this kind of activity to be annoying because it was such a frequent distraction to teachers and students, Annette still felt as if she had "died and gone to heaven" in Horizon Valley. After all, she had great students, a good salary, a wonderful, modern school building, and resources that allowed her to do many things in her classroom that she had only dreamed of earlier in her career. With all the benefits, it was surprising one day to be summoned rather abruptly to the principal's office. When she arrived, Dr. Carson, the principal, noted that he was quite concerned by a recent note that he had received describing a parent's concern over how "the new fifth-grade teacher" seemed to be "too busy" to talk to a very committed parent.

Apparently, the complaint was based on a situation that occurred about a week earlier. Annette had been working with small groups of students engaged in science projects around her classroom one day when Mrs. Danielle Davies, president of the local PTA, stopped in to visit. She pulled Annette away from one group of students and asked to have "just a few minutes" of her class time to talk to the children about the visit she was planning to the Horizon Symphony Orchestra next month. Annette politely asked Mrs. Davies to come back in a few days; today was devoted to the science projects and preparation for the science fair for the school tomorrow night. Mrs. Davies smiled and said that she understood, then left the room. Now, Annette was asked to explain to the principal why she was so "rude to an important supporter of the school."

When Annette left the principal's office, she needed a few minutes to clear her head. She went to the teachers' lounge to get a cup of coffee. She was clearly disturbed by the meeting she had just left, and Donna Spencer, a fourth-grade teacher who had spent the past twenty years in the school, came over to see if Annette wanted to talk. After hearing the story, Donna smiled and said, "You'll learn about this place the same way I did. The parents seem very active, involved, and supportive. But there are some pretty big egos here. Don't be surprised if you keep getting attacked for one thing or another. It goes with the turf here in Horizon Valley. This is a good district, but you always need to be aware." Annette left the lounge and started to wonder who would help keep her aware of any future land mines.

In what ways could a mentoring program for veteran teachers have helped Annette in her transition from one school district to another?

_____

_____

_____

_____

_____

Describe some of the ways in which teachers who have experience and who come to your school or district are provided with information and support as they start their jobs in your system:

_____

_____

_____

_____

If this list is blank or you must admit that your district does nothing to help veterans who come on board, do not be surprised. Very few school districts across the nation do anything to help with the transition problems faced by experienced teachers coming into a new setting. The prevailing model is one that suggests that if you have done it somewhere else, you already know all of the answers. "That's why we hired you—so you won't have to bother anyone with questions," is an implied statement related to why some experienced teachers are selected rather than beginners. This image is wrong and denies the fact that people often find ways to learn about new cultures, norms, practices, and expectations as they proceed from one school system to another during their careers. After all, it is not a case of simply stating that "a school system is a school system is a school system."

Consider another case. Martin Quinn has been an English teacher at Henry Ford High School, a large school with nearly 3,000 students, for nearly twenty years. He has spent his entire career at the school. In short, he has spent a lot of time with the other teachers and knows the district, the school, and the community.

Martin certainly knows about his school and its environment. However, seeing and knowing people in work settings does not always allow a person to really understand his colleagues. What is even more frustrating to Martin is his belief that none of his coworkers know much about him or appreciate his work, goals, or professional dreams. For years, he has known that teaching can be a very lonely job, but now he feels as if he is becoming alienated from any real contact with his peers.

How could a mentoring program provide support for Martin and help him feel less isolated?

_____

_____

_____

_____

How could a mentoring program in your district help serve the needs of experienced teachers?

_____

_____

_____

MENTORING FOR
EXPERIENCED TRANSFERS

Throughout this book, a vision of mentoring for both beginning and veteran teachers has been presented. Clearly, a different vision is needed for experienced teachers who transfer to a new school or district; they are newly hired teachers, but they have experience in other school systems. You might assume that the issues that are associated with initial socialization to the profession of teaching would have been addressed during the earlier phases of a person's career. A person who has been a teacher in one school district will likely already know the "feel" of a classroom. But unlike beginning teachers, transfers are probably not going to experience many problems with role identity and perhaps only limited difficulties with the technical demands of the job.

On the other hand, many areas that are covered in a mentoring program for rookies can also be addressed to transfer teachers, particularly such things as initial orientation to a new school system and remediation of specific skills that are needed for performance in a new school district. No matter how long a person might have served as a teacher in another school district, he or she has probably never worked in the new school system before. For example, even if a person has had extensive experience and training with the use of certain instructional technology in some other setting, those practices might not be completely compatible with what is now done in the new system. As a result, someone who can show the newcomer "how we do it around here" can be quite helpful.

It might be necessary to provide needed information to an experienced teacher in the following areas:

1. What they are expected to know about instructional technology and how to learn more if there is a problem

2. Orientation to the vision of effective teaching and student learning that has been adopted by the new school system

What are some of the specific areas in which mentors might be able to assist experienced teachers who are newcomers to your district?

_____

_____

_____

MENTORING FOR
VETERANS WITHIN A SYSTEM

Mentoring programs for beginning teachers are based on the assumption that those who are new to a school or some other organization do not have all of the experience, knowledge, or basic skills that they need to do their jobs at the same level as others who are already in the same system. As opposed to the programs for rookies or even transfers, which address issues associated with a need for initial professional socialization or orientation, mentoring for veteran teachers is cast in an entirely different light. This last model of mentoring must be seen as a peer coaching strategy that would encourage pairs of teachers to work together in order to promote more effective, ongoing professional development.

In what ways do you anticipate being able to make use of peer coaching when guiding the professional development of veteran schoolteachers?

_____

_____

_____

_____

CHECKING YOUR PLAN

The last two chapters looked at how you might develop teacher mentoring programs that are targeted at the specific needs of two different groups of school leaders: beginners and veterans. Chapter 2 suggested that an important part of your planning process would involve deciding the exact nature of the target group to be served by your mentoring program. Review the following list of planning items to see how your planning has gone so far:

A. Will your mentoring program be directed exclusively at the needs of beginning teachers in your district, or will it be available to all teachers?
_____ Yes _____ No

B. Is there a clear understanding of the kinds of issues that need to be included in mentoring programs for beginning teachers (in contrast with topics that are more appropriate for veterans)?
_____ Yes _____ No

SUMMARIZING THE CHAPTER

This chapter provided information concerning the possible applications of a mentoring program that focuses on the learning and developmental needs of experienced schoolteachers in your district. There are two groups of experienced teachers: (a) those who are new to your system but who have had experience in other districts, and (b) those who are experienced teachers in your system.

Some of the important issues to be remembered when working with veteran teachers in a mentoring program are the following:

- The mentoring program cannot be perceived as evaluative in nature.
- Mentoring should be arranged in order to maximize peer-coaching strategies rather than organized as implied hierarchical arrangements in which the mentor instructs the protégé.
- The program will be more difficult to sell because many experienced teachers have been socialized to the belief that they must never admit concerns to their colleagues.
- Despite the previous statement, mentoring for veterans is important because most school leaders, when questioned individually, admit that they often feel lonely and isolated in their roles. Mentoring is a way to reduce these feelings.

Did the Mentoring Program Work? 10

Planning for and implementing a mentoring program for school-teachers—whether for only the beginners or all of the teachers in the district—implies that a considerable amount of time, effort, and financial resources will have to be invested in a new activity. It is reasonable to expect to see some degree of accountability as part of the program. Part of your initial planning for the adoption of mentoring should involve serious thinking about how you will know whether what you planned to do has actually been achieved.

This chapter offers some suggestions for developing a framework that will enable you to determine whether all of your hard work has been worth it.

EVALUATION QUESTIONS

As a school district tries to determine whether or not its mentoring program is successful, it might wish to review the following basic questions:

Was the program effective? This question asks whether or not the program appeared to meet the goals and objectives that were selected in its initial development. According to this criterion, how effective has your program been in addressing the goals and objectives that were first identified by your district mentoring planning team?

_____

_____

_____

A number of different strategies can be used to help you answer this question in your school system. For example, you might wish to design a survey questionnaire that asks those who have been involved in the mentoring program (either as mentors or protégés) to rate how effective the program was in meeting its stated objectives. Or, it might be possible to conduct interviews of program participants to determine their perceptions. This step in the evaluation process is quite obviously dependent on the extent to which the goals and objectives that were first stated for the program were clearly stated and realistic.

How expensive was the program? What costs were incurred as a result of the new mentoring program? For example, was it necessary to carry out special inservice and training sessions? Did you have to hire external consultants to help with the development of your program? How much time was spent on developing the program?

How much did the new mentoring program cost your school district to plan and implement?

_____

_____

_____

As you respond to this question, remember to take into account the expenditure of nonmonetary resources (such as time). It is nearly impossible to determine whether the cost of the program is completely worth it, but you should be able to know how much you have spent in the areas of program planning and implementation.

Did the program meet the needs of all participants? Again, this situation is difficult to judge objectively, particularly if you have a large number of mentors and protégés who are participating in your program. Nevertheless, it is important to try to determine how those who were mentored and those who served as mentors perceived their experiences.

How well do you believe your program met the individual learning and developmental needs of the individuals who participated by serving as mentors and protégés?

_____

_____

_____

As noted previously, you might design a questionnaire to be distributed to all teachers, or you might wish to interview those who were directly involved in the program. Both techniques will give you useful information to help you decide if your hard work appeared to be worth it (at least, in terms of stated criteria).

Did your mentoring program meet the needs of your school system? Remember that good mentoring can serve as a "value-added" feature of a school system; it has the capability to add something to the school system in which it is developed and implemented. To what extent do you believe that your mentoring program helped the district meet its needs?

_____

_____

_____

The best way to respond to this question is to examine the mission statement or operating philosophy of your district as a whole and decide whether or not the mentoring program was in keeping with these statements. You might also wish to look at the goals and objectives of the school board for this year, the superintendent's goals, or the stated professional development objectives for the school system.

Did the program really help the protégés? Chapter 1 listed some of the common benefits of mentoring programs, as expressed by those who have been mentored. Has your program achieved some of these objectives?

What are some of the perceived benefits achieved by protégés in your school system during the past year?

_____

_____

_____

Again, the principal way in which you can get answers to this question involves talking directly with those who were the beneficiaries of the mentoring process. You might wish to interview all of the teachers who were mentored during the past year to determine whether their personal and professional goals were achieved as a result of the mentoring program.

Was the overall school system helped as a result of the mentoring program? In short, did you find that your school district was more effective in achieving many of its goals and objectives because the mentoring program was in place to assist teachers? Was it a better place for children to learn and grow because mentoring was available for the school district's teachers? To what extent did the adoption of a mentoring program in your school system improve the overall quality of the district?

_____

_____

_____

As you respond to this question, think about not only the intended ways in which the quality of your school district was improved after you planned and implemented the program, but also consider some of the unintended ways in which your school district has become better (or worse) after having started the mentoring program.

Have you addressed program weaknesses as well as program strengths? There is often a tendency to focus on those features of a program that have worked exceptionally well. To get a complete picture of the effectiveness of a program, you should also recognize areas that can be improved in the future.

What are some of the areas that you believe your program needs to improve in the future?

_____

_____

_____

If you have identified certain weaknesses in your program, you need to take action quickly in order to ensure that these types of concerns do not destroy your efforts the next time the mentoring program is offered in your district.

Were participants in the program provided an opportunity to work together as a way to grow professionally? Remember that one of the main goals of implementing a mentoring program has been to reduce the sense of isolation that is traditionally experienced by teachers. Did you unintentionally add to this feeling by keeping mentors apart from one another? Did you enable protégés to get together as a group?

In what ways did your program promote collegial relationships among all participants?

_____

_____

_____

Something that might be obvious but is often overlooked is that everyone needs support from others. In other words, do not forget that mentors also need mentors—and those who are mentored do not always need the direct intervention of their formal mentors. They can also learn and grow as a result of contact with others who are in similar situations.

Did you allow ample opportunity for program participants to provide input into the overall assessment of your program? Have you listened to those who are on the firing line? In what ways have you accounted for ongoing input from program participants as a way to improve the mentoring program in your school district?

_____

_____

_____

It is critical for people who are involved with any activity of professional development to have input into the design, structure, and ways in which that activity is carried out. Mentoring for schoolteachers is not an exception to that rule.

A few additional thoughts are offered concerning effective assessment practices to be applied to your review of the mentoring program in your school district. Any effective evaluation program will provide evidence of the following:

- Collaborative efforts
- Participant involvement
- Well-designed planning activities
- A practical, well-designed delivery system
- Attention to local implementation issues

CHECKING YOUR PLAN

How well do your mentoring program and its strategy for evaluation measure up to criteria that are identified as part of the planning process?

A. Phases of program evaluation
  1. Context evaluation
     a. Is there a plan for identifying environmental factors that might affect your mentoring program or its outcomes?
        _____ Yes _____ No

     b. Does the plan include methods for measuring the effects of these factors on the mentoring program and its outcomes?
        _____ Yes _____ No

     c. Are there provisions for determining whether the program needs assessment has correctly identified the needs of mentors and all teachers in the district?
        _____ Yes _____ No

  2. Input evaluation
     a. Are there provisions for evaluating your written program?
        _____ Yes _____ No

     b. Are there provisions for evaluating the appropriateness and adequacy of human and material resources that are assigned to the mentoring program?
        _____ Yes _____ No

  3. Process evaluation
     a. Are there provisions for determining whether the mentoring program has been implemented according to your stated program goals?
        _____ Yes _____ No

     b. If any components of the mentoring program have not been implemented according to your program plan, are there provisions for identifying the lack of implementation?
        _____ Yes _____ No

      c. Are there provisions for identifying the effects of the lack of implementation?

      _____ Yes _____ No

   4. Outcomes evaluation

      a. Is there a plan to measure whether or not program objectives have been met?

      _____ Yes _____ No

      b. Is there a plan to measure positive and negative unintended program outcomes?

      _____ Yes _____ No

   5. Are there provisions for analyzing data from each phase of the program evaluation and for synthesizing the results of that analysis in a comprehensive evaluation report?

      _____ Yes _____ No

B. Are there procedures for reviewing the mentoring program in response to the program evaluation?

   _____ Yes _____ No

C. Are human resources identified in order to coordinate and implement program evaluation and revision?

   _____ Yes _____ No

D. Are material resources identified that are necessary for program evaluation?

   _____ Yes _____ No

SUMMARIZING THE CHAPTER

No matter how strongly you might wish to protect and keep any program, it is always necessary to make certain that your wishes are supported with some evidence that the program was worth it. Whatever that value is, maybe you can identify the worth in advance before critics find their own criteria for assessment. As a result, this chapter strongly urged you to make certain that a clear and rational evaluation plan is firmly in place prior to your implementation of a mentoring program for schoolteachers in your district. Failure to follow this step will likely lead to the failure of your hard work over time.

Moving Beyond Starting Your Mentoring Program 11

here is a great tendency, whenever energy has been expended on a particular topic, to relax soon after that effort is completed. Planning for and implementing a mentoring program for the teachers in your district represents such an activity. As stated throughout this book, program planning and development require a lot of hard work on the part of many different people. Those who are actively involved in the program as mentors and protégés must spend a considerable amount of time and energy on their work if the program is to be effective. After one year, there can be a tendency to breathe a sigh of relief and simply let the next year happen. Unfortunately, that kind of attitude will do little to ensure that all of the current year's hard work will return many benefits to your school district.

One of the most disappointing things about program development in education in general, whether it involves new curriculum teaching practices or professional development programs, is that it is often viewed as a process that has a very short life span. Experienced educators are well aware of the fact that in certain school systems, change is represented by a series of gimmicks that seem to come and go every year. It is not unusual to hear educators reflect on activities in their school systems in terms of which programs lasted how long and in which years ("Last year, we did Total Quality Management, and the year before that, we were into site-based decision making"). Both the lay public and professional educators are faced with an endless and often bewildering array of disconnected activities characterized by jargon and buzzwords. It is therefore not surprising that many innovations in education do not seem to have much of an impact on improvement, and this situation results in understandable skepticism and cynicism on the part of many school people.

When adopting a mentoring program for the teachers in your school system, you should consider the program as only a small part of a total professional development program for your instructional team. There are numerous cases of school systems embracing the concept of mentoring as some sort of an ornament to be added to the activities of the school district without much thought of how they will fit into the total scheme of support for classroom teachers. In those cases, it is not surprising to find that the mentoring program has not survived beyond a year or two. The answer to the question of what to do after mentoring must be based on a serious review of the overall vision of professional development in a school system.

HOW DOES PROFESSIONAL DEVELOPMENT FIT?

An unfortunate but well-known reality is that when times are tough in a school system (e.g., when funding is reduced), one of the first activities to disappear is support for staff development and inservice education. Many people recognize that such a stance is shortsighted, but little is done to change things so that there is both a recognition of professional development for teachers and that the program is more than some sort of frill.

One of the reasons why the public might have such a negative view of the importance of professional development activities for educators is because we rarely spend time articulating in our own minds the purposes and priorities that are associated with learning programs for the adults in our schools. It is critical for any district to periodically review its vision of developmental activities for its teachers and then base its program development on this vision. After that is in place, it might be possible to add a mentoring program or any other type of special activity that is dedicated to the improvement of teaching and learning.

REVIEWING LOCAL PRIORITIES

To begin the process of determining what is being done at the local district level for the professional development of schoolteachers, it might be helpful to think about local responses to the following questions. This process might be viewed as similar to the development of an educational platform for a school district:

1. What is your vision of effective teaching in your district?

2. What is your local district's vision of school effectiveness?

3. What are your expectations regarding the ways in which teachers will be a part of the local vision of effectiveness?

4. What is the relationship between existing priorities for the school district and new initiatives in professional development for your district's teachers?

5. How does your program for teacher professional development overlap or connect with ongoing district organization development?

The great concern is that a district might simply initiate mentoring for teachers as an add-on program that has no real connection to daily life in a school system. It cannot be viewed as something that is a luxury (without any real impact on those essential features of schooling that are related to student learning). Not only will the public be offended by such a vision, but also teachers themselves—as clients of a mentoring program—are not likely to support activities that detract from the time that is available for the primary task.

WHAT HAPPENS AFTER MENTORING?

Another recommended course of action to ensure that mentoring is not a kind of add-on activity that is unrelated to the essential activities of a school system is to work out a way to make certain that the mentoring program will persist. You can perform this task by establishing a structure to support the maintenance of mentoring in the future.

One example of such a structural support is the institutionalization of the mentor role as an ongoing position in the school system. Districts often designate a few teachers as mentors for a year, then identify others to serve in this role in the next year of a program. Mentoring in such a context becomes viewed as a rotated honor, rather than as a core responsibility to be carried out by those who have special training and expertise. Mentoring is hard work, and it should not be used as only a type of ceremonial reward for a teacher with a record of long service to a school district.

Another recommendation is that once you have established certain teachers in your district to serve as professional development mentors, you need to make an effort to bring these individuals together on a regular basis in order to maintain enthusiasm (and again, to institutionalize the role of the mentor). Part of the time that is spent in the sessions can be devoted to social events that focus on the needs of teacher mentors to interact with others in similar roles. Part of the time can also be directed toward learning activities that will help practicing mentors fine-tune their skills.

What might be some additional ways in which your district could provide ongoing support for those who are designated as mentors?

_____

_____

_____

CHECKING YOUR PLAN

Review your responses to the following checklist to see how well you have planned for life after mentoring in your school district:

A. Mentors
   1. Are provisions made for formal and informal mentor needs assessments?

   _____ Yes _____ No

2. Are provisions made for modifying mentor training or mentor support as a result of the mentor needs assessment that is administered during the first year of implementation?
_____ Yes _____ No

B. Are human resources identified in order to coordinate and implement mentor needs assessment and corresponding modifications in the mentoring program?
_____ Yes _____ No

C. Are material resources identified that are necessary to carry out mentor needs assessment?
_____ Yes _____ No

SUMMARIZING THE CHAPTER

This concluding chapter was designed to help you think about what the next steps will be after you have initiated a mentoring program for school-teachers in your district. There is often a great tendency, based on all the hard work that is associated with the initial program implementation, to forget about the need to build long-lasting support for any innovative effort. It is absolutely critical that you do not waste your efforts by not deciding in these earliest stages to commit your district to a lasting vision of professional development. That is the true value of what has been presented throughout the chapters of this book.

APPENDIX A
Answers to the Mentoring Background Quiz in Chapter 1

1. **False.** Effective mentoring programs are designed so that both protégés and mentors benefit as a result of mutually enhancing positive interactions and support.

2. **False.** Those who have spent more time in a certain role are not necessarily more effective in that role. That is, they are not automatically better mentors. Besides, there is more to mentoring than simply showing another person how to carry out a certain task.

3. **True.** Effective mentoring should help people grow professionally and personally.

4. **True.** Research shows that, particularly in education, women tend to place a higher value than men on types of interpersonal relationships. This statement does not mean that men cannot or will not benefit from mentors who are women, or that all women are necessarily effective mentors, however.

5. **True.** Those who participate in a mentoring relationship one time are likely to serve in similar programs in the future. Also, those who are mentored tend to become mentors to others in the future.

6. **True.** The essence of effective mentoring is that it must involve the development of mutual trust and commitment on the part of both the mentor and the protégé.

7. **False.** Because of the complexity of most professional roles, it is likely that a person will need multiple mentors during his or her

career. Such a practice will also reduce the likelihood that a person will develop too great a dependency on only one individual.

8. **False.** No interpersonal relationship, particularly one that is as intensive as an effective mentor-protégé relationship, will be so perfect and smooth as to involve no conflict at all.

9. **False.** There are many ways of matching mentors and protégés. Making use of similar job titles and job descriptions is one approach but is certainly not the only effective strategy that can be used.

10. **True.** Many different benefits can be derived from an effective mentoring relationship.

11. **True.** Mentoring can involve a number of different professional development activities that are negotiated between a mentor and a protégé. Mentoring is not solely a one-to-one conversation between a mentor and a protégé.

12. **True.** There are many different and important relationships available to school leaders, such as career guides, peer pals, and so forth.

13. **False.** Mentoring is based on effective performance on the job.

14. **True.** Because mentors and protégés often form extremely powerful bonds, it is easy for expectations to be high. Nevertheless, it is critical for both partners to remain realistic about the nature of their relationships.

15. **False.** The most effective mentors are those individuals who engage in a process of discovery with their protégés. Effective mentors are able to ask the right questions but are not always able to provide all the right answers.

APPENDIX B
Mentor-Protégé
Action Planning
Form

Protégé Name: _____

Mentor Name: _____

Three major goals for this year:

1. _____

2. _____

3. _____

Objectives	*Learning Activities*	*Outcome Measures*

SUGGESTED READINGS

Bova, Breda M., & Phillips, R. R. (1984). Mentoring as a learning experience for adults. *Journal of Teacher Education, 35*(3), 196-210.

Daloz, Laurent A. (1999). *Mentor* (2nd ed.). San Francisco: Jossey-Bass.

Janas, M. (1996). Mentoring the mentor. *Journal of Staff Development, 17*(4), 2-5.

Jerome, Paul. (1994). *Coaching through effective feedback.* Irvine, CA: Richard Chang.

Keirsey, David, & Bates, Marilyn. (1984). *Please understand me: Character and temperament types.* Del Mar, CA: Gnosology Press.

Kerka, S. (1998). *New perspectives on mentoring* (ERIC Digest No. 194). Columbus, OH: ERIC Clearinghouse on Adult, Career, and Vocational Education.

Kolb, David A. (1984). *Experiential learning: Experience as the source of learning and development.* Englewood Cliffs, NJ: Prentice Hall.

Kram, Kathy. (1988). *Mentoring at work: Developmental relationships in organizational life.* Lanham, MD: University Press of America.

Lawrence, Gordon. (1982). *People types and tiger stripes: A practical guide to learning styles.* Gainesville, FL: Center for Applications of Psychological Types.

Murray, Margo, & Owen, Marna. (1991). *Beyond the myths and magic of mentoring.* San Francisco: Jossey-Bass.

Myers, Isabel. (1962). *Manual: The Myers-Briggs type indicator.* Palo Alto, CA: Consulting Psychologists Press.

Pitton, Debra Eckerman. (2000). *Mentoring novice teachers.* Arlington Heights, IL: Skylight Professional Development Press.

Portner, Hal. (1998). *Mentoring new teachers.* Thousand Oaks, CA: Corwin Press.

Portner, Hal. (2001). *Training mentors is not enough.* Thousand Oaks, CA: Corwin Press.

Reiman, Alan J., & Theis-Sprinthall, Lois. (1998). *Mentoring and supervision for teacher development.* New York: Longman.

Rowley, J., & Hart, P. (2000). *High performance mentoring.* Thousand Oaks, CA: Corwin Press.

Sweeney, B., & Johnson, T. (1999). *Mentoring to improve schools.* Alexandria, VA: Association for Supervision and Curriculum Development.

Zey, Michael G. (1991). *The mentor connection.* New Brunswick, NJ: Transaction Publishers.

INDEX

Action planning form, 81
Action, empowering protégés, 47
Advancement (career) and mentoring, 16
Advising, 26
Age of mentor/protégé, 40
Assessing program. (*See* Evaluating
    mentorship programs), 69-74

Beginners, inexperienced as target group,
    53-62
    issues faced in first year by, 57-59
    needs of, 59-60
Benefits of mentoring, 3-5
    to mentors, 3
    to protégé, 4-5
    school systems/district benefits, 5

Career advancement and mentoring, 16
Characteristics of mentors, 23
Communication skills, 23
Cost of mentorship programs, 73-74
Criticisms of mentoring programs, 5

Danger signals in mentors, 25
Development:
    human relations skills, 31-32
    professional, 75-76
    program (initial), 9
    needs assessment for, 9
    planning the program in, 9
    rewarding and supporting mentors, 35
    role and responsibility assignment in, 24
    selecting mentors, 23-27
    target group identification in, 13-14
    team effort in planning for, 8-9
    training mentors, 28-37

Effectiveness characteristics in
    mentors, 20-23
Effectiveness of programs, 69-74
Empowering protégés for action, 47

Establishing limits in mentor/protégé
    relationship, 48-49
Evaluating mentorship programs, 69-74
    benefits of, 2-5
    checklist questionnaire for, 73
    cost of program, 73
    effectiveness of program in, 72-74
    goals and objectives of program
        in, 69-71
    participant in put for, 9
    questions for, 9
    strengths of program in, 72-74
    weaknesses of program in, 72-74

Forms, action planning, 81
Framing issues in mentor/protégé
    relationship, 48
Functions and duties of mentors, 24

Geographical proximity of mentor, 40
Goals and objectives of mentoring, 13-14
    career advancement in, 16
    future objectives and programs in, 77
    identification of, 13-19
    professional development and, 74-75
    reviewing priorities and, 9-12
Groups (targets), beginners, 53-57
Guidance (career), 16
    role of mentors, 24

Hires (new) as target groups, 53-57
Human relations skill development, 31-32

Implementing mentorship programs, 8-10
Importance of mentoring, 3
Initial program development, 8-10
Issue identification in mentor/protégé
    relationship, 48-49

Key issue identification in mentor/protégé
    relationship, 48-49

Limits, establishing in mentor/protégé
     relationship, 48-49
Listening skills in mentoring, 26

Matching mentors/protégés:
     age of mentor/protégé and, 40
     criteria for, 20
     gender issues in, 40
     geographical proximity of mentor/protégé
          in, 40
     goals of, 13-14
     myths of, 39-40
Mentoring defined, 3
Mentoring skills development, 33-34
Mentors:
     action planning form, 81
     assisting mentors, 35
     career guides as, 26
     characteristics of, 20-24
     functions and duties of, 26
     listening skills in, 26
     negative characteristics in, 25
     observation skills in, 26
     problem-solving skills in, 26
     protective function of, 48-49
     rewarding and supporting, 35
     training of, 28-37

Need for mentors, 1-2
Needs assessment for program
     development, 8-9
New hires as target group, 55-57

Organizational level of mentor/protégé, 40
Orientation to mentoring in training
     programs, 28

Planning mentoring programs, 1-2
Priorities of mentoring programs, 13-14

Problem-solving skills in mentoring, 49
Professional development and mentorship
     programs, 76
Programs, mentorship, 8-11
Promoting self-directed learning, 49
Protective function of mentor, 49
Protégés:
     action planning form, 81
     age of mentor and, 40
     benefits to, 4
     empowering of, 48
     establishing limits in relationship, 48
     framing of issues with mentor, 48
     gender of mentor and, 40
     geographical proximity of mentor to, 40
     matching with mentors, 38-43
     organizational level of mentor and, 40
     protégé defined, 4
Purpose of mentoring, 1-3

Reading (suggested), 83
Rewarding and supporting mentors, 35
Role and responsibility of mentors, 26
Role modeling, 25

Selecting mentors, 23-24
Sharing experiences, 48-49
Skills:
     ability of mentors and, 24
     development function of mentor, 25
     listening in mentor, 25

Training mentors, 28-37
Transfers and veteran teachers, 66-67

Veteran teachers:
     as target group, 66-67
     checklist questionnaire for, 67
     transfers and new situations for, 67

**CORWIN
PRESS**